A CURIOUS IMPULSE

© MACW Press 2009

All rights reserved. No part of this book may be reprinted or reproduced or utilised by electronic, mechanical or other means, now known or hereafter invented, including photocopying and recording, or any information or retrieval system, without permission in writing of the publishers.

Published by MACW Press
Printed by Brunswick Press

ISBN 978-0-9562851-0-2

We gratefully acknowledge the financial support of the School of English, Drama and Film UCD, and the following sponsors:

Abbott
A Promise for Life

THE CLARENCE

A CURIOUS IMPULSE

An Anthology of New Writing
from the
MA in Creative Writing
University College Dublin
2009

24 Sept 2009
To Phil,
Love from Claire x

Acknowledgements

The UCD Creative Writing MA class of 2009 would like to thank the following people:

James Ryan, Éilís Ní Dhuibhne, Harry Clifton and Frank McGuinness for all their guidance, and for making the MA a hugely beneficial experience; Edna O'Brien, Adjunct Professor of Creative Writing at UCD, Mary O'Donnell, Claire Keegan, Deirdre Madden, Kevin Power and Hugo Hamilton for the inspirational advice they gave us throughout the year – hopefully we've put some of it into practice! And we would also like to thank Nicholas Daly, Head of the School of English, Drama and Film UCD; Hilary Gow; the McKillen family; Brendan McAtamney; Denise Bevan; Annemarie Ryan. And finally, everyone who assisted us in the production of this Anthology.

Foreword

J 207: Day One: September 2008

"We better not begin yet, it's only ten to."

There are eight, perhaps nine people seated around the expansive table. Three or four to come. I glance about, smile.

"Ack no, I've not written that much…"

"Me? Well – I have this novel. It's set in Cork. Mostly." Expression – unbelievably trusting.

A voice from down the table filters through; "On and off for years, if the truth be known. I'm hoping this course…"

And another, "Poetry, mainly." She seems set to continue – but doesn't.

A girl in a redder than red coat comes in. Is parking always this difficult on campus? An icebreaker. The lady with early Nana Mouskouri glasses comes alive. So too do three or four others. Common ground. Parking. Yes, Parking. Terrible. Common ground turning to quicksand as quickly as it had formed.

All return to GO.

Not a word from the fellow with the just-got-up hair. Or from the fellow across the way from him, looking quizzically at everything and everybody.

"No, this is booked for the morning." A voice from the corridor, growing louder. The door opens a little, a face appears. "Sorry." All heads swivel, then swivel back.

"New Jersey – sort of..." I look in her direction. The application profile suggested intellectual rock chick. Wrong call?

Nothing on that September morning, not a stir, not a rumble that might have signalled the avalanche that was already in train way up the mountain. In what seemed like no time at all that group went from pathologically quiet to explosive; ideas flying here there and everywhere at cartoon pace – not enough time to say all there was to say.

We knew full well just how talented they were when we read the submissions that accompanied their applications. What we could not have anticipated was just how much they were going to learn from each other. This anthology, this rich, diverse, sparkling anthology is a great testimony to the talents of its twelve contributors, but equally and perhaps more laudably it is a testimony to the highly charged, positive interaction that made this a wholly admirable class.

And the avalanche rolls on.

James Ryan

Introduction

In the continuing and, one fears, never ending debate about the merits of Creative Writing programmes, a point on which there is some agreement between the opponents and the supporters of the cause is that the one thing you can't give apprentice writers is imagination, whatever else you might be able to teach them. That's the gift that they must bring to the table themselves – that spark of life, the gift of nature or the gods, or of lucky genes.

What immediately strikes me about this anthology is that it sparkles with imagination, and imagination's companions: energy, originality and love of language. From the dark ironies of Jamie O'Connell's 'Daisy', the plain girl with the dancing grandmother who tells her compelling story from an unquiet grave, to the light-hearted surrealism of Jennifer McGrath's 'Boterique', the anthology dances along with a freedom and vivacity which lifts the heart of this grateful, and happy, teacher.

Tania Tynan's astonishing story of a girl who grows the ghost face of her father over her own, Anne Graham's darkly bizarre 'Jesus Christ Pose', Claire Coughlan's completely fresh take on the concept of the moving statue, are all stories which depart radically from the realm of realism while containing, somewhere in their shimmering and often violent layers, the grain of truth which is at the heart of all good fiction. These new writers are not playing safe; they are taking risks, experimenting with form and idea and words. They are flexing their literary muscles and plunging into the ocean of storytelling with unusual courage and plenty of style.

The more realistic fiction in the anthology is equally imaginative and the best of it is breathtaking. Here we have new writers who know how to mix humour and tragedy, quick witted irony and deep psychological insight, and writers who can also weave and twist words with the consummate skill which is the hallmark of the true artist: Colin Barrett performs this alchemy in 'The Dynamiters of Quebec', a profoundly felt and fully realized story, in which the perspective of a young boy is expertly captured; so does Mariad Whisker in her passionate, sharply poignant 'Tangled Up in Blue'. Susan Stairs' beautifully modulated dissection of bullying in a marriage in 'Leaving Traces' is as delicate as it is shocking; Anne Coughlan gives us a heartbreakingly evocative memoir, where the entire lives of a mother and two daughters are caught on one day in the 1960s, preserved forever in what Alice Munro has called the 'lovely clear jelly' of fictional memoir.

Several of the prose writers write a poetic prose, layered and rich in imagery. The poets in the class write with similar enthusiasm, and, as the stories have poetic qualities, many of the poems have narrative aspects. Caroline Dowling's delicate lyrics tell stories of weaving and sewing, modern domestic relationships and dilemmas; John Taylor's 'Belfast Flâneur' series is a robust, invigorating story of a true poet in love with his city (and I'm glad to say he has one Belfield poem, the only one I have so far seen, ever, coming from the Creative Writing programme in UCD!). Jennifer Brown's highly accomplished, perfect poems narrate fascinating stories of love, clothes, outings to the zoo, journeys – she is a poet who has the imagination to see the worth in every living, and inanimate, thing.

There are stories and poems in this anthology which strike right at the heart of what it means to be a human being. And there is writing in this student anthology which is excitingly promising, as well as writing already mature, professional and accomplished, which will always be a credit to its authors, whatever the future has in store for them. But what is evident above all is the freeing of the imagination which this class of 2009 has allowed itself. Such freedom and open-ness could not have been achieved without a generosity of literary spirit. And this generosity imbues the anthology. It is as if all the writers had taken the advice of Jennifer Brown's poem:

> 'Let the wind wrap around your legs
> ...Don't question, just absorb it,
> just live it, just let it glide you through.'

What we have here is creativity, in the best sense of the word.

I am very proud to have been associated with the class who wrote and compiled this collection, and produced it with such care. Imagination cannot be taught. But it is great to be around when it leaps into action. And with such grace.

Éilís Ní Dhuibhne
1 July 2009

XII A Curious Impulse

Contents

Jamie O'Connell □ *Daisy* — 1

Tania Tynan □ *The Ghost Face* — 13

Caroline Dowling □ *Home Ground* — 27

Susan Stairs □ *Leaving Traces* — 39

Colin Barrett □ *The Dynamiters of Quebec* — 51

John Taylor □ *Belfast Flâneur* — 65

Anne Graham □ *Jesus Christ Pose* — 77

Anne Coughlan □ *To Hell with Poverty, Let's Kill a Chicken* — 87

Mariad Whisker □ *Tangled up in Blue* — 97

Jennifer Mary Brown □ *These Hours in the Cellar* — 109

Claire Coughlan □ *Maria Maria* — 121

Jennifer McGrath □ *Boterique* — 131

Notes on the Writers — 143

Jamie O'Connell

Daisy

When I was alive I never amounted to much. I would've liked to have been someone but I wasn't very good at anything. I didn't quite fit in either. I wasn't tall, thin, or beautiful like Amy Markston or Sarah Whitmore. I was average. Plain. That's the awful thing about it.

Being average and shy amounts to the same thing as not existing. No one bothers with you. You are invisible.

The blood has stopped flowing out of my head. My heart stopped beating about five minutes ago. The ambulance will arrive shortly and they will try and revive me. But it won't work. I'm already gone. Maybe I'm what I always suspected – truly invisible. I wouldn't mind being dead if I had just saved him. But even in that I have failed.

His cool hand touches my ear, the arm of his jacket soaked in my blood, our blood. I wonder where he was first hit. He looks alright; his beautiful face is undamaged though his neck is oddly bent. Maybe he broke his spine as the truck threw him against the traffic light. Or it might have been the knock to his head as he hit the metal post.

We will lie together for the first and last time. For ten minutes. He will be buried in a family grave in Kildorrery. I'll be dumped in a plot outside the town with a headstone in the shape of a heart. Fifteen miles apart. Yet, we will always have now. It will have happened. For ten minutes I will be happy. For ten minutes, I will exist.

◻

"Your dinner's in the fridge."

She'd left a note on the hall table. The house was grey when I opened the kitchen door. The bronze handle was smooth and cool to touch. I took the key and placed it back under the third flowerpot on the windowsill.

I liked the silence in the evening. I flicked the heating switch on the wall. It was an old Georgian house and the pipes groaned a little, creaking into life. It took ages to heat the rooms, but the high ceilings were worth the sacrifice. My mother had a fur overcoat, and I would wander down the three flights of stairs, elegant, reposed. I had a fascination with clothes dragging on the floor behind me – capes – it just seemed so very grand. Flump, flump, flump as the heavy fur dropped from step to step.

Before she died, Nana lived with us for two years, occupying the top floor. The room smelt of talc and orange disinfectant. She had a little television on an old dresser, on which we watched her musicals. I dreamed of being adorned in the colossal dress that Debora Kerr wore in *The King and I* – the impracticality of it. She was an ornament, a piece of moving china to be adored. Every door in the palace had to be ten foot wide to fit the floating silk. Or to be Molly Brown, saving hundreds on the Titanic, singing, wearing sapphires that shimmered and sparkled with effervescent light.

Nana would dance with me. Twirling, singing and laughing, suddenly vibrant. She could waltz, teaching me the steps. "One two three, one two three…" The panelled walls faded into marble, the light drifting in the window, a spotlight.

I wonder why it is at either end of life that people dance. Nana always danced; I always danced. Mam and Dad never did. Even at the end, when Nana couldn't get out of bed, she smiled as I drifted along, lost in my dream in which I was a porcelain star, beautiful, spinning, like a doll in a music box. Turning around and around on a magic top.

The world spun more and more violently as she grew still and cold, leaving the house in a brown box. A packaged doll returned to her creator, faulty, why else would she have stopped and left? The films mocked. I stopped watching them.

I was Miss Havisham, sporting my fur coat, which still flump, flump, flumped on the stairs – a rhythm. It felt like my own heart stopped beating around that time. I hadn't read the book but Mam had the DVD and I watched it again and again. I didn't care for Pip or Estella. Their stories were not mine. But Miss Havisham had a grandeur of her pain. I enjoyed the agony she gave me. All her beauty and soul gone, yet she remained striking, notable, utterly remarkable. I could be her. I could be totally miserable. Then people would notice.

I broke biscuits over the kitchen countertops and floor, lay on the tiles in the fur coat and red heels, while the Labrador, the Yorkie, the parrot and two hamsters wandered free, gobbling up the wedding feast around me. I spread out my hair on the tiles, like a banshee. I would starve myself so that I could feel the groan. And I cried for Nana.

☐

"Bold lover, never, never canst thou kiss, though winning near the goal – yet, do not grieve. She cannot fade, though thou hast not thy bliss, for ever wilt thou love and she be fair." I remember those words. Keats. 'Ode to a Grecian Urn'. To be forever loved. Forever admired. But she was fair and I was not.

The bus used to pass by our house, and from that moment I had three minutes to run outside, while it turned around and made its way back. I jumped over the modern cattle grate and waited by the giant monkey puzzle tree. Hopping on the bus, I took my usual spot by the window, two rows back.

Loud, they were all sitting on the rear seats. Amy was immaculate, smooth brown hair, layered; white straight teeth and a laugh that travelled up the bus. Sarah was shorter with more curves and blonde hair – the school Monroe. I wondered did Amy or Sarah ever worry about the day they would walk into a room and no-one would see them. When they would be old.

For now they ruled. Though I heard the other girls complain about them, I knew it was simply jealousy. Because I was jealous – to be them for just one day. To have someone just look at my face and be smitten. Maybe if someone else saw it in me, I might be a bit more convinced.

They had their own challenges. I overheard them once, sitting behind me in the classroom, "He wants me to give him a blow job…" Amy sighed. "Tell him to go fuck himself."

No-one sat in the seat next to mine until the rest of the bus was filled. I was weird. I placed my bag on it, making it less obvious I was alone. It was black canvas with beige leather edging. I sometimes spoke to a couple of the other girls who went to a different school.

They were nice, though not having the same friends made it difficult. Our microcosms of existence were different – being from another school was like being an alien. Besides, they were always talking about *Sex and the City*, which I was never allowed watch. I'd seen it once at my cousins' house, so when we discussed which of the characters we were I was relieved not to be caught out. Not knowing the right stuff made you a retard, and *Great Expectations* didn't count.

"Oh my God! I'm so Carrie!" Amy butted in.

"No, you're Samantha, ya whore!" Sarah laughed, wandering up the bus, deftly jumping over the schoolbags.

Of course they never asked to be part of our conversation. They naturally assumed it was their right and we remained unquestioning. They were like the sun, which for the most part was hidden behind the clouds, but every now and again would burst forth and interrupt our lives. And we would enjoy the warmth of their glow. Though this could be closely followed by a bitter mockery. Most of the time I think they just saw us as novelties, creatures in tanks to be poked at. Certainly not equals.

We never questioned this fact either.

"So who are you? You've got to be Charlotte." Amy was talking to me. I flushed, uncomfortable with the attention.

"I… I guess."

Amy placed her knee on the spare seat next to mine, gazing down at me. Sarah leaned over the head rest. I could feel myself shrinking.

"So who'd you fancy anyway?"

"Sorry?"

Amy glanced at Sarah.

"You ever shifted anyone?"

"I…"

The two of them burst out laughing.

"So, do you ever finger yourself?"

I felt nauseous, and unable to say a word.

"Come on, 'fess up. You fancy Mark?"

Mark was sitting three rows behind, his headphones in.

"The fucking homo and the lesbian! A match made in fag heaven!" They both laughed. Most of the bus stared. I tried to hold back the tears, feeling light-headed, feeling like I was going to choke.

"Amy…"

It was Karl. He sat on the back seat of the bus with the others. Blond, athletic, funny and popular. Pip. They turned away from me and wandered back down the bus. I was saved and utterly grateful for this apparent good luck. As they walked back down the bus, he glanced at me. Concerned.

The look lasted for a second. He turned away. I blushed. No one else had noticed. He had called them away, saving me. The mortification vanished in an instant. I felt a glow of gratitude. Tears formed in my eyes and I blinked, holding them back. The two girls behind looked at me, probably thinking they were tears of embarrassment. They weren't; they were tears of happiness. Overwhelming thanks.

He'd saved me. Deliberately. Kindly. Not wanting any appreciation. He had noticed me, seen beyond the plain face, the normal brown hair, the 'averageness'. Realised I was a person. Real, breathing, that I had blood in my veins that bled when I was cut, flesh that bruised when I was hit, and a heart that ached a little bit more every day.

□

Looking back, I wonder did I put too much emphasis on one moment, one look. Maybe I had got him wrong altogether. He never approached me afterwards. The rest of the week passed without anything being said. The pang became unbearable. Alone at home I wondered why had that been *it*?

I dreamed of him. In the silence of the living room I gazed at the mouldings on the ceiling, thinking, fantasising. I played a silly game. Rather childish really, it was called, *How Much do you Love Him?* where I would dare myself to do things to prove that I loved him completely. To show that I was grateful. There was nothing else to do anyway.

I stood at the top of the stairs, suddenly nervous. It had seemed like a good idea lying on the carpet. I felt scared. But I had to know. If I had the choice, whether he had to fall down the stairs or me, would I love him enough for me to do it? I closed my eyes, my heart racing, and I leaned forward, taking a deep breath through my nose. I let go of the balustrade.

I don't remember it hurting. I woke up at the bottom of the staircase, my legs tangled into the mahogany telephone table. The telephone had fallen onto the black and white floor beside my hands. Red and green light from the stained glass on the door flickered on the tiles.

As I got up, I ached. I really ached. My right shoulder especially. But it was an ache I endured for him. So I didn't mind. I had proven it. That I would hurt for him gladly. That I would die for him. And it paid off. The stars, God, or whatever controls the fates, saw that I passed the test.

☐

"Don't take any notice of Amy."

Karl was alone in the corridor. I was walking the other way. I couldn't look at him. He called my name and I froze as he asked me whether I was alright. His light blue shirt was open, inside was a rugby jersey. I glanced at his blonde hair, short, curly and those blue eyes, full of intent.

"I… yeah…" words fell out of my mouth.

"*Hey Karl!*"

His stupid friends, Pat Hurley and John Connor appeared around the corner. He looked at them. My legs felt weak. Karl smiled and walked off, not saying anything else.

"*What are you doing talking to that fucking freak? You know she…*" Pat's words echoed up the hallway, vanishing as they disappeared around the corner.

It was a perfect moment, just too short. He had cared. But I hadn't said thank you. I hadn't let him know. I'd fucked it all up. I was undeserving. Maybe if I tried again.

☐

I slowly dragged the knife across my forearm, clenching my teeth, realising if I did one more cut I might get another chance to speak to him. I couldn't risk it not happening, so I just cut and cut, trying not to cry out. That would make me weak. I would be brave. Prove my love for him. People had been tortured much worse than I had. What was I complaining about? If I could get him, I'd have everything. I would be a person. Real. If I could just speak.

But no amount of cutting would work; week on week passed and nothing. We never spoke. I even tried the stairs again. But I had failed. It was my fault. I hadn't been enough. Just so fucking average. A nobody. Insignificant. Then he changed school and I didn't get to see him again.

☐

Tonight was a cold night. I had just finished work. Two evenings a week in an internet café. My mother didn't approve. She said she'd rather give me the money. But I didn't want it. Neither had Nana. The more I remember, the more I realise she hated their kindness, knowing it was a burden to them. Them whispering downstairs about who would bring her dinner, like it was a monstrous chore. They wouldn't even walk up the stairs to help her.

Selfish. I hated them. I would never be a burden to them, not as soon as I could pay my way.

My God, it was cold outside. I wrapped the black scarf around my neck. My hair had been surprising me all week, now jet black. I knew Mam hated it. That's why I did it. Not because I liked it. I still had the memory of the porcelain Debora Kerr and waltzing with Nana.

As I crossed the square I saw him for the first time in three years. Just beyond the rows of headlights and noise of traffic. Under the large town clock. He was laughing with his mates.

They were all drunk. He hadn't changed, except the light blue shirt was now blue and white stripes, and the grey pants now denim.

I wanted to see him close up. So I walked quickly, looking at my phone, to make sure it looked like an accident if we bumped into each other. After all, I wasn't a stalker.

Then I saw Sarah. She kept touching his arm, clinging onto him, smothering him. Now, I could never talk to him. He didn't like her doing it, his brow tensed with her laugh. I knew his every gesture like they were my own.

They were drunk. It was stupid. Like cattle knocking into each other as they were herded up the street. One of them shouted something about Tom's Nightclub. A miserable place I had gone once and avoided ever since. Maybe I would go there.

At the back of the group, near me, John hopped on Pat's back and they raced up the street, charging into the group. And they all laughed. Until Pat slipped and John fell sideways, pushing Karl into the road. None of them noticed. Karl wobbled on the tarmac. I saw the truck.

So I ran forward and jumped. The scars on my arms had trained me to be fearless. I didn't mind pain. I welcomed it, just wanting him to live. Sarah screamed. The lights of the truck blinded me. A beep. And that was it.

So that's where I am now. Lying in the street with him. We remain together, man and wife. Our blood mixed as one. In a way I am sad because I have failed him. I didn't get to save him as he saved me. I hope he forgives me because I did my best. It just wasn't enough. It never was.

I probably wouldn't have told you this if I was alive. I would have been too shy, too embarrassed. Even now, there are one or two things I wouldn't admit to. Yet I have my love story. I have my happy ending. Being here with him, contented with the man I have always loved. The next twenty minutes of my death will be my life. I shall exist, as people gaze at us together. Then I shall go into the ground, and like Nana, I shall sleep.

Tania Tynan

The Ghost Face

Isabelle was a pretty child. She would dress her cats in bonnets and bibs, bring them outside into the longer grass by the lower garden-shed where she created a school, a church and restaurant tables for them and for her dolls, to eat special muck dishes garnished with daisies. In school, her students were skilled at drawing. They each had a small neat copybook sitting on their lap with an appealing drawing at the top of the page and news of when Isabelle's father was coming home again in tidy lines beneath.

Elizabeth Kitty would sit still, accustomed to her mantilla, and purr only when she had to as Isabelle said mass. Isabelle wore white towels about her body, a T-towel on her head and large wooden rosary beads tied as a belt. Young and devoted, she read from her father's prayer book, pausing occasionally to straighten up Lily's missalette and stop Elizabeth Kitty cleaning Manny's face too much.

Michael, Isabelle's father, died when she was thirteen. At his wake, her auntie Elaine said to her, "Good God, Isabelle, you're the absolute image of your father, d'ye know that, Chicken." It was true, the resemblance was uncanny. She had always looked like him, more so than her mother. She had a very good relationship with Michael and although he was not a young man, his death came as a shock. His affairs lay unsettled: he had clearly intended to see his youngest girl grown up. Isabelle grew serious and brooding on his passing.

In the flurry of the funeral, relatives and strangers stopped and held Isabelle and whispered to her and cried in her ear: "What a clever man your father was; he was widely read, your father; perhaps too clever for his own good; a fine man; an intelligent man; a man who died before his time." He had read the *Encyclopedia Britannica* and the *Oxford Dictionary*; had a photographic memory and could learn them off by heart A through Z; and could do *The Times* crossword in a flash.

Isabelle couldn't do a crossword: words didn't come quickly to her. She could read and picked up her *Children's Britannica* at 'A' and started to keep her father alive in the only way she knew how. She took to reading a lot. As time passed, the family didn't speak of Michael to the child. They progressively didn't speak to her much at all. She became invisible to them.

Her two older sisters, Sylvie and Anne, still lived at home, but only just. Upstairs was hectic when they got ready to meet their boyfriends, only to become desolate when they were gone on their dates, leaving Isabelle to finger through their make-up brushes discarded in the bathroom.

Within a few years of Michael's passing, the older ones moved away, one by one, but without much time in between. Their different rooms became empty and stopped being known as 'Anne's room', 'Sylvie's room' and 'John's room': instead her mother called them the blue room, the green room and the yellow. The room for Theresa, the woman who helped, became empty too, then, called the red room. With the extra space, her Mother, Mary-Margaret, allowed her own things to sprawl and fill into their old space.

In her teens, in her own room, Isabelle examined her young face closely in the mirror. It was stiff. The colour was definitely older than her years. Around the jaw had become jowly. There was looseness about the skin that once held her girl's eyes up and bright. Sag occurred. There was a slight red rim under her eyelid. It was the stiffness of the skin that most perplexed her. She cupped her face and felt it. It was different from her neck, which was soft and slender. She liked to look at her back. It was thin and shapely and her skin looked a pale pink there. She often stared over her shoulder at her back but tried not to see her face as she did this, but instead the curve of her spine at the nape of her neck. That part of her was still pretty and feminine.

Like other teenagers, she got acne on her face: huge pustules on her nose and forehead. It made her look a little masculine.

Mary-Margaret had enjoyed dolling Isabelle up as a child. She bought her daughter the prettiest dresses and coats and would put her hair in ribbons. When her friends gathered for drinks on a Sunday afternoon she paraded the young girl around and would receive profuse confirmation of her excellent taste and generosity as a parent. Increasingly, after Michael's death, her teenage daughter irritated Mary-Margaret without meaning to. Isabelle's mannerisms reminded her of her late husband. She was always reading and often used a turn of phrase the way the old man did. The teenager looked at her mother with the dead, sullen eyes of her father and often, Mary-Margaret could not even bear to look at her. She lashed out in frustration and venom at her daughter that the old man was not gone. "Why, he'll never be dead while you're alive!" she'd scream at her.

Lonely at home and unable to understand the upset she seemed to cause her mother, Isabelle took to spending long hours alone upstairs. Out of boredom, she took to gazing in the mirror and drawing her reflection. Watching herself, she was reminded of her father. She saw his rough stubble in the shadow beneath her jaw and the heaviness of his brows over her now small, sunken eyes. She lifted the charcoal up to her upper lip and drew a moustache over her mouth, digging into her flesh. She was startled at the recognition. Her father's face stared back at her from her own image, his ghost inhabiting her face. "It's you, Daddy!" she said to her reflection letting the charcoal drop to the bare floorboard. "Yes," he answered, "It's me."

She finished drawing the picture, her hand shaking. Her teeth grew sore from clenching. The portrait was dark and foreboding;

the crosshatching was too rough and heavy to be naturalistic. It wasn't him, she decided. She heavily imposed the lines for her own long hair.

At night, Isabelle wore her father's striped pyjamas to bed. They were much too big for her, as her father was a large man, but she drew the cord around her tiny teenage waist. She often lay as still as death and woke in the morning, little rested, without so much as having stirred once in the night. She had idolised her Daddy in life. He called her his little 'Beauty.' She believed everything about the man to be without fault or compare.

To school, she wore his wrist watch because she felt it would help her in exams. She practiced her handwriting till her 'T's' and 'I's' were like his. Leaning out the window of her bedroom onto the flat roof, she played the tune he would play on the flute. These were the only belongings of his she had, and she treasured them. Mary-Margaret had Theresa throw everything else out shortly after the funeral. Isabelle had rescued his whistle and his sheets of music from the bins outside.

Drawing herself again, late one night, the ghost face spoke to Isabelle for the second time. "It's me. It's Daddy!" it said. This time, the girl didn't look up. "You're not afraid of your Daddy, are you?" he asked. Isabelle was upset and afraid but she shook her head and whispered "No." "No. That's right. We're one now. My face is in yours. You recognise me, don't you?" he asked. Nervously, she lifted her head up. The ghost face looked dour; uglier than ever before and older, much older than her youthful visage. She felt tears hot on her own face but didn't see them on the face of her older, distorted reflection. She saw her shoulders shake under the face in the mirror. The tears caused them to crumple in and over and her school blouse quivered below her jumper. The ghost image was taking over hers.

She left her room and crossed the hall to Mary-Margaret's room to show her the self-portrait. The door was half open and she could hear her mother inside, bustling through her wardrobe.

"I can't find the skirt for my blue Basler jacket," she said. "Is it in your room?"

"No," said Isabelle. "Why would it be in my room? None of your clothes are in my room."

"Well, Theresa put it somewhere, will you go look in the green room, it must be in there?" She continued, "How do these shoes look?" She picked up a pair of navy and white high heels.

"Fine," replied Isabelle, uninterested.

"Don't you care how your mother looks? Don't you want your mother to look nice? Go look for that jacket in the green room."

Isabelle held her charcoal drawing up for her mother to see.

"What's that?"

"It's me."

"No it's not," her mother retorted, "That's not you. Why, that's dangerous looking!"

Back in her room, with her door locked, Isabelle studied the drawing. It did look just like her and was as ugly as her face had become. The strokes were rough and jagged. The paper was a dull shade of grey and the dark drawing stared out with ugly, disgusted eyes. The grimace on the cheeks and mouth held Isabelle in contempt. She asked out loud of herself, "Why is the ghost in my face?" She wondered why she had lost her own pretty face. What had she done wrong?

She craned her chin into the bathroom mirror and pulled at her cheeks, and watched her mouth stretch. She knew that her own face was missing; gone from her. She experimented with Mary-Margaret's make-up, particularly to see if her eyes would appear as her own as they used to. "Was there, in fact, a change at all?" she asked herself again incredulously – it was all so hard to believe. She was forgetting who she was, just as her mother and sisters had forgotten her. She could no longer see her own potential to become a beautiful woman. The ghost face had gained ground in putting forward his image in her and stomping out her young loveliness. Her innards felt dead. What was the point?

People kept saying: "You look just like your father. You are the image of your father. You're the image of your Daddy." Her face had become increasingly like her father's yet it was darker, menacing and heavyset. The family was aware of the girl's dark alteration, but reasoned that the teenage years were transformative and in Isabelle's case unfortunate, rather than cause for concern. Anne, her sister, was more sensitive and conscious of the girl's suffering. She knew Isabelle was stricken by grief whereas the other family members had managed to motor single-mindedly through their bereavement. She offered advice on medicated moisturisers but was embarrassed to highlight what she feared might be a natural ugliness and silenced herself and then appeared to ignore the girl's problem altogether.

Isabelle became more immersed in her dark condition and her behaviour darkened in accordance. At night with her comb, she would pull the stiff flesh of her face down; pressing the metal teeth in until they left an imprint of tiny red dots. She hacked into a pore and pulled it. After scraping a neat little tear, she put salve and gauze on the cuts as she slept at night in her father's pyjamas. The scrapes and nail prints partially healed and smoothened during the night. With her fingernails she pressed into her palms and up along her inside arm.

She laid out old photos from her past on the floor. In an early picture, she was a new born baby in the summer time. Mary-Margaret looked sweet and proud and wore a sleeveless dress with large white flowers on it. She was smiling up at the camera and Isabelle, the baby, appeared to be smiling too. Her baby self had floppy arms and looked like she didn't have a care in the world. In the next image, she was with her father. She was a pudgy, blonde toddler scooped up into her father's strong arms. The two of them were laughing. Something was so funny that their eyes had gone into their heads and their bodies were both almost doubling over. The next photo showed Isabelle with her toys. Some of them were nearly bigger than she was and they all seem to be immersed in a picnic together – a sociable group of colourful characters out on a rug on a sunny day. As Isabelle fondly passed through the years of different photographs, she noticed a marked difference in her appearance at puberty. At thirteen, she had changed. She pieced together that she hadn't had her face, as she knew it, since she was thirteen, when her father died. A thought struck her; maybe he was living on through her face. It seemed so. Then, where was her own face gone?

At sixteen, she went looking for her own lost face. She spoke to her mother. Her mother didn't believe that there was a ghost in her face and merely told her just to smile more. She looked for her face in the faces of others, on the bus, in magazines, in cafés. Once or twice she thought she caught a glimpse of it in the reflection of a shop window or in the rear view mirror of a car. She practiced approaching mirrors differently, either with a grimace or a smile – hoping the ghost face would be taken off guard to allow her grace to see her own for a second. She felt her face still existed somewhere even if no-one else could see it – this, she accepted. She knew the important thing was not to lose sight of her belief that it was somewhere and that she would get it back.

As the years passed, the ghost face weighed her down. At eighteen, her cheeks drooped low. The jowl sagged half way down over her neck. "You are not part of me!" she wept at her reflection. "Come with me!" replied the ghost face. "Why live so unhappily here? Come with me! Come with me and be free of the weight of living here." The ghost face half closed his eyes and moved his head from side to side. "Come with me!" he taunted.

She knew killing this part of her would be a way of laying the ghost face to rest. She also knew she risked killing more than just the ghost face in the process. Weighted with sorrow, she accepted this and summoned the energy to act. With a knife, she peeled at the reflection in the mirror. It didn't budge. The ghost's eyes simply followed the edge of the knife as it scraped on the glass. She put the knife to her own face, in under her ear to tug at her jaw. The ghost face stared on. The skin of her jaw was as tough and stiff as hard leather. Cutting into it didn't yield blood. Instead, she needed to jut the knife in with force to gain a grip. It slowly and stiffly tore her skin. With her free hand, she grasped her nails into the cut skin and pulled. It didn't rise up much; it was so tough; like the leather of an old saddle.

Her mouth was stretched wide open, yet only small gasps of pain came out. The skin came away and the pain of it seized her body into a terror. In the mirror, the ghost reflection looked steelily on; he looked at her pulling the hardened flesh away and not into her screaming, terrified eyes. "You are not part of me!" wept Isabelle. Blood started to dribble along her jaw and drop from her chin. It trickled at first and then like an opened clot started to swell over her face like a cloth contagion. The ghost looked into her eyes and said "Isabelle!" She could hardly hear him. "Isabelle!" the voice got louder. "ISABELLE!" he warned. "Go to your mother!" His eyes penetrated her. "Go to your mother! Tell her. Ask for help! Ask her for help, Isabelle!"

Seeing the ghost face with compassion in his eyes frightened Isabelle even more. She screamed. She screamed and screamed and screamed. Covered in her own blood, she passed out on the floor.

Mary-Margaret was at the door at the bottom of the staircase when she heard the horrific sound. She panicked. A strange sensation of her dead husband ran through her and made her very afraid. "Michael! What is it now?" she breathed and her legs took her upstairs.

□

Isabelle's body lay motionless on the operating table. Mary-Margaret stared in through the glass panel of the theatre door. She was terror stricken and would not let anyone near her. Isabelle's sisters, Anne and Sylvie and her brother, John, sat patiently close by. There was a silence among them. They dared not speak and strained to listen to the sounds from the doctor's theatre.

As the surgeons peeled the masklike flesh from her, they were visibly shocked, not alone by the hide-like unusualness of the flesh but also by its cool temperature. The bleeding stopped on the girl's arrival to the hospital. After an initial wiping, the surgeon was unsure of the tonal quality of the skin. Its leather-like texture and thickness perturbed him. He was reminded of the image he had seen, once as a student, of the Bog Man of Tollund. The girl was alive and in shock but her proper recovery, he felt certain, lay in the removal of the thick deformity of excess skin from her face. It constricted her breathing and she was rightly terrified by it. He pared the skin back and felt like the skin had gone down the ages. It was at times like a layer of bog oak in quality. Once, not quite knocked out by the anaesthetic, the girl spoke incoherently. She said her father's ghost face had inhabited hers since she was thirteen. Paranormal occupation was not something the doctor believed part of our experience when we are mentally well. He worked for hours and in his own mind felt like an early witch doctor rooting out a spirit; clearly influenced by the girl's talk in her mental delirium. When he had finished, she fell quiet and her flesh, peeled back to an early dermis, was raw and visually arresting.

She slept for hours and eventually woke up looking like a new born, with placenta all over her face and head. She was covered in a wet dew of sweat.

"What is it, Doctor?" asked her concerned sister and mother of the senior doctor. "It's a rare psychological phenomenon. The worst I've seen. It's like the pressure of a patient's mind can cause a reaction where the face then proceeds to quite literally and physically bury itself." He rubbed his own forehead quite fiercely as though not knowing what to say next or how to say it. He stared at them head on and then quickly shook his head to the left and proceeded decidedly, "The scarring will not be permanent." He thought silently and said, to conclude, "Some emotions find no other way out." He continued to the nurse who was approaching and walked with her, "Yes, there are a few skin grafts above the eyes; minimal stitching under the brow; paper stitches in the cheeks. She's young, her flesh will heal with freshness, and a new beauty will emerge." The nurse ticked boxes on her charted board and nodded seriously and knowingly.

Entering Isabelle's hospital room, a young doctor explained, "She has new eyes now; new eyes to see you with." Isabelle's eyelids fluttered as she heard the doctor and her family enter the room. The young doctor carried a hand mirror and held it gently up for the girl to see her new reflection. Shakily, she leaned up to look and saw a head covered in neat dressings. Without seeing much actual skin, she saw her eyes were wide as they stared back at her. Her cheekbones had symmetry. Her nose was small and straight and the hollow of her cheeks had a perfection and attraction to it. "You have lovely bones, my dear," said the young doctor, "the raw material for loveliness there just waiting to be uncovered." Isabelle had a moment of disbelief for she couldn't feel any heaviness on her jaw or brows. She looked curiously and admiringly into the little, shaky, hand-held mirror and nodded respectfully to the doctor, whom she saw reflected as he leaned encouragingly behind her.

To recuperate, Isabelle spent time in her sister Anne's house. The house was on the mountain. It was a fresh beginning for the girl. Her married sister had a baby who was curious and touched Isabelle's dressings gently as she healed. Isabelle felt more connected up here. Her mother came up for tea every day and her brother, John and sister, Sylvie called frequently too. The only image of her father was in a framed picture on the mantle. It was a nice picture of him, at home, in the garden. Every time she passed it, Isabelle stroked the picture fondly and whispered, "You have no power over me anymore!"

At night, Isabelle lay beneath the roof window staring up at the stars. She was free of dressings. The nurse told her to simply let the air at it, and in time it would be a healthy colour and the scars would fade to tiny thin lines. Isabelle felt her own face was back. It was different, mature of course, scarred of course, but beautiful. She was beautiful in her own way. One night, when she fell asleep, she had a vision; it was the last time she would see her dead father. The ghost appeared, kind now, to tell her a message. He said: "We are relatives, who are a mystery to each other through death. Living relatives are a mystery to you by not relating to you in life. We are all 'lives' – dead or alive – to relate to each other, even though it may be hard. Relate to your relatives, Isabelle, even though they may not deserve it. Do not hate them."

Her scars healed. Thin layers of skin shed to reveal a new, better flesh beneath. She recognised herself again and felt a new energy inside. On the mountain, she had her choice of ways to walk. She could go out back, up-hill through the gorse into the rough fields with the sheep, or down to where the old military range was. On a clear day, she could see islands out on the horizon. Even on a bad day, it had to be very overcast not to see the villages of North Barrow stretch out before her. She could make out the exact location of all the different steeples and follow the main roads with her eye into town. She had made friends with the postman, with Michelle from the lower house and when her sister's baby got over her cold she went for a walk down to the nearest little shop with her in the pram.

Caroline Dowling

Planting

A heel shove
shunt to the shovel
shifts the shaft
inches in
turns back
the strip of garter

grasses coiling
the surface,
revealing
beneath
the naked
moist opening

where I place
a single polished
seed head
hard
as a ball bearing
into the marriage bed.

A sprinkling
of waters pulse
starts the partners,
peals the bluebells
plumes pink petals of
cherry blossom confetti.

At this green altar
I am witness
to a marriage.

Tomato Plants

When I brush past
The young tomato plants,
Head and shoulders
Thriving in their grow bag

In the greenhouse,
Our flesh dress touch
And scent cheers
Promises to come

Of sweet plump fruit
Rolling the air.
As if to say,
We know what we are

What we will be.
So accepting
So certain
Of their destiny.

Pruning the Heather Bed

She came up through
the membrane of moss
blanketing the peaty earth
in the heather bed.
I had her in my bare hands
gripping her woody hair,
a wiry bloomless wig
of wayward growth.

I dug in my muddy heels
struggling to release
the growthy glut.
She slucked loose
from the sodden sod
her head a clump of clay
her hair a matted crown.
Centuries of shared secrets

slipped into the autumn sunlight.
I had an urge to unravel
her ancient locks,
comb them through,
clean the dirt caked features
free the tongue-tied mute
make her my companion.
Reach a common ground.

A sister, of soil and seed and sediment.

Redress

Deceit scales the trees.
Fibrous festering scabs
frock skin tight and shroud
bole and bark and bough

suffocating flesh that weeps
the green sap of itself
through fault lines.
Trunks leak light's milk

nipples to a tacky dribble.
Shoots break out and harden
lunging new life. Calloused
crusts fall to feet of clay.

Grandmother

You are a weaver of cloth.
Your loom is yourself.
White hands shuttle the warp
and the weft of your frame.
Bobbin bound like your belly
you grow out to grow in.
Crisscrossing you lace strands
over and under through
tricks and traps
hoops and loops
snaring and snagging
until your yarn is
licked through the eye of
the needle by love.
Spinning out of sight
you spool sky and earth
cords of yourself.
Taut to weave
magic on life's fabric
you turn your hand
to living tapestries.

Mother

Stitches tack and hem
our patchwork home.
The bodice of your dress
the box pleats of your skirt
starched shirts
collars and cuffs.
Rugs to bless the cold
floors of our beds.
Embroidered quilts
dream catchers
like the figures living in
your golden eiderdown.
A young girl's hair
is a minute shell
two chain stitches
her slanting eyes
hands joined, elbows bent
she faces her partner
in a bell shaped dress.
Each corner of the quilt
tells a new tale.
Figures in a garden
at a tea house
under a blossoming tree,
one thin running stitch
connecting all episodes.

Guest

Copper pots and pans cling clang
clean on the granite counter top.

Tonight you are cooking
up a symphony, a feast of

pealing metal scaling the kitchen
cupboards and crockery in frantic

efforts to conduct a well timed
tasty supper. While for once

I sit a guest at our table
sipping a Bordeaux, smiling as I watch

you boil and burn and blunder. The food
of love filling the blue night air.

Marriage

Your suit case
skites the bare boards
of the corridor
in the half light
of dawn.

Your suited shadow
swallows me up
as you stoop
to deliver
the goodbye

see you soon
taxi's waiting kiss.
Off you go
on your
executive mission.

No word or kiss
can keep you.
Absence fills
the loss account
of us. Waiting we

grow bankrupt.
Reporters in our own
story we relay news
of minor milestones
down the hotwires

of our mobiles. We
skype each other to
connect long distances.

Together when apart.
Apart when together.

The drip, drip, drip
of absence. The now
you see me now you don't
face of fatherhood.
Marriage by instalments.

Susan Stairs

Leaving Traces

Chris pulls a blue and white carton from the recycling bin and places it on its side on the chopping board. He takes the meat cleaver from the wooden block and chops down hard on the carton's middle, tossing the half that says *Organic* back into the bin. He washes the remaining dregs of stinking curd from the bit that says *Low-Fat*, running the hot tap into the sink until all the sour milk disappears down the plughole. He dries his hands and folds the tea towel, placing it back on the marble draining board, then passes out through the open French doors to the patio.

It's nearly ten and heading towards darkness. Behind the branches of next door's eucalyptus tree, the sky is a sprawl of bloated pink clouds against a smear of inky blue. Laura sits under the striped parasol. She has turned on the lamps that double as heaters. Their red-orange brilliance spills across the slats of the hardwood table and down over the Indian sandstone flags.

On the table is an open bottle of Shiraz and the remaining two of the set of four crystal glasses that were a wedding present from Laura's office. Chris had reduced the set to three when he knocked one to the kitchen floor last Christmas morning. The look on Laura's face had almost ruined the day. Last week, one had broken while she washed it in the sink. "Three was a stupid number for a set anyway," she'd said to Chris. "We won't miss it. It's not like they were Waterford or anything."

Chris disturbs the air around the yellow citronella candle on the table, as he sits down facing his wife. The flame wavers, almost dies, flares up bright again. Under the lights, Laura's thin, white arms look golden, just like after their holiday in Sicily last year. Sitting out in their tiny sheltered garden at this time has been a nightly ritual for them all summer.

"Did you find something to put them in?" she asks.

"Yeah, this'll do," Chris shows her the sawn-off carton. "I'll start collecting them in a minute."

He sinks back in his chair. Laura pours them both some more wine. The air at night is beginning to cool. It's almost September. The countdown to autumn has begun. The scent of the clambering jasmine they planted when they first moved in comes and goes on the night breeze. Chris closes his eyes. The outline of Laura's body pulses yellow-white behind his lids, like the scorching mid day sun when you've looked at it too long. He wishes the image would disappear.

Back when they'd first met, he wanted to see her all the time. He conjured up pictures of her in his mind when they were apart, scribbling sketches while he was on the phone at work – mini portraits in blue biro that he couldn't bear to throw in the bin. They were all still somewhere in his desk, stuffed in drawers between stacks of unread reports.

It hadn't been like that today. Today, he didn't want her face in his head. When he tried to think of something else, there she was, her blue-green eyes like stagnant water. Resolute. Unmoving.

"I can't believe the amount of damage they've done." Laura looks around the garden.

"Mm. They're hungry buggers," Chris opens his eyes, drains the wine from his glass. "Must be all the rain we've had. Draws them out."

In the darkened corners, where the lamps' light cannot reach, the shiny, dark-green leaves of their Japanese aralia plants wave out of the blackness. Giant, outstretched hands, wanting to be clasped and held. Rooted in cobalt-blue glazed pots, Chris and Laura had thought they were Castor-oil plants when they'd seen them in the garden centre. "A common misconception," they were told by the assistant. Chris had wanted evergreens. "I hate when stuff dies off in winter," he'd told Laura. So they'd bought bamboos and grasses, the jasmine and two aralias.

All the plants had flourished in their pots on the sheltered patio, but the vigour of the aralias' growth had surprised them. Leaf after leaf had unfurled its fingers, tiny baby fists at first, stretching out and growing bigger than dinner plates. They'd grown out as well as up, each one now over five feet tall, three feet wide. Sometimes, Chris stands at the French doors and looks out at them, marvelling at the rate of their progress, taking pride in the fact that they've done so well.

But lately he's noticed something's wrong.

Holes have started to appear on the outermost leaves; a lacy pattern of tiny bite marks bleeding together to make gaping spaces in the green.

"I don't know why we can't just get the pellets," says Laura. "It'd be so much easier."

"For us maybe. But not for them. And if birds eat the dead ones, they get poisoned too."

Laura examines her French manicured nails. "Always have to do everything the hard way," she sighs, scrutinising each one in turn.

"Hard way's always the right way."

Chris runs his finger round the rim of his empty glass. A deep desire for a smoke envelopes him. It's been almost a year. "A sign of pure love," he'd told Laura, "I've known the fags longer than I've known you." He'd done that the hard way, no cutting down or weaning off them for weeks and weeks. Smoked his last one the night the clocks went back last October. "Now is the winter of my discontent," he'd laughed the next morning. He'd expected things would happen as a result of his decision. It was one of the steps, one of the things couples do in preparation; give up the fags, cut down on the nights out, eat healthier food, get rid of the cat – not that they have one. Laura's allergic. If next-door's tabby so much as sneaks along the garden wall, her eyes start to water.

"Did I tell you Brian and Helena are having a boy? She had one of those 3D scans. Brian's over the moon." Chris' words fall like china cups on concrete.

Laura looks closely at her palms.

"Have you seen my Norwegian formula? Can't find it anywhere. My hands are so dry."

Chris pushes himself up from his chair, allowing the metal legs to scrape noisily across the ground.

"Better get started on this then," he announces. He flip-flops over to the nearest of the aralias, his bare leg brushing off Laura's knee as he passes. She picks at the dry skin on her hands.

"Think I'll go up," she says. "I'm in Cork tomorrow. I need a good night. You'll be a while doing that anyway." She slips her feet back into her strappy gold sandals and clicks over the flags. "Don't forget the lights." she calls back, "Forgot to tell you they were still on this morning when I came down. Can't wait to see the effect of that on the bill."

Earlier this evening, when they'd first come outside, Chris had examined the leaves again. The holes were bigger. After all his nurturing, his aralias were in danger of being destroyed. He couldn't understand it. He'd sat down under the lights, drinking his wine in silence, Laura flicking sharply through the latest copy of *Heat* magazine, licking her right thumb before turning each page.

Then, he'd seen them.

Moving down the smooth walls in a slow procession toward their verdant Mecca. An army of slugs. Some coal-black, big as sausages; smaller ones like strips of liver.

"There's your answer," he'd told Laura.

"To what?" she'd asked, her head lowered over a page of shoes and bags.

"Slugs! Would you believe it? I was sure it was something with wings, something making a getaway as soon as we'd come out. They must have been here every night. How could we have missed them?"

"There you go. You can't always see what's right in front of you. Get some pellets on your way home tomorrow."

"I'd rather just gather them up, put them out in the lane. Eddie threw a heap of weeds out there the other day. That should keep them happy."

Laura had said he was mad, needed his head examined, to be gathering slugs in a container when pellets would do the trick in no time. Chris couldn't bring himself to do it. That's why he's squatting down now, gently easing a fat one into the sawn-off carton with a twig. He finds baby ones too, concealed right in under the smaller leaves, probably left to feast there all day while their parents hide under pots and in holes in the wall. He moves around the plants methodically, turning the leaves to the glow of the lights, carefully unfolding the fingers of the tinier ones, in case anything is hiding inside. It's not long before his container is full. He opens the gate in the back wall, carefully tipping the slimy stack of yielding bodies into the pile of weeds. Then he goes back for more.

Music starts up from somewhere, the *tzud tzud* of a backbeat to a tune he recognises but can't place. He finds he enjoys nudging the slugs off the leaves, takes pleasure in his personal mission. He thinks he might like to study horticulture, spend his days in the outdoors instead of stuck in the office jungle behind an oak-effect desk. Why does she feel this way? What's wrong with her? He finds a whole cluster, huddled on top of each other for comfort, as if they're waiting for him. They fall into the container in one plop. It's natural, normal. It's what couples do. She thinks too much about it. It'd be better if it just happened. And she won't even talk about it. There you go, you fat little beauty. And your baby too. Sorry guys but you'll have to dine elsewhere tonight. And she strings him along, feigning that despondent look every month when she tells him it hasn't happened this time.

Maybe he goes on about it too much, puts her off with his ardour. He should give her more time. Like when they first met and she didn't seem so keen until he backed off a bit. No more juicy leaves for you, I'm afraid. It's time for a change of diet. Maybe he should have guessed. She never seemed that pushed about babies, now that he thinks about it. Never made a fuss over them. After five years skirting around the issue, she'd finally laid her cards on the table last Saturday night, on the way home from her mother's birthday dinner. Chris was driving.

"Don't think Kate and Tony are getting much sleep at the moment," he'd said, tightening his grip on the wheel. "Harry's teething. Has it quite bad they said, poor little fellow."

"For Christ's sake, Chris!" Laura had almost screamed. "I get the picture."

Chris had fixed his eyes on the orange tail lights of the jeep in front. He stared at them without blinking until they were far too close and he had to jam on the brakes. The silence in the car was like an air bag between them. Growing. Swelling. He felt he would suffocate. Without thinking, he'd swerved right, across the path of an oncoming car, and down a narrow street in the direction of the seafront. Pulling up alongside the harbour wall, he stopped the car. Watching the clock on the dash, he waited a full minute before jumping out.

The strength of the night wind coming in from the east had caught him off guard, whipping the door from his grip, walloping it shut. Great gusts blew into his face, stripping the moisture from his eyes, stealing the breath from his lungs. To steady himself, he leaned into the waist-high wall and for one crazy moment saw himself jerk the bulk of his body over the top. He looked down. The drop was deep, probably twenty feet, into black frothing waves that slapped themselves up against the smoothened concrete. His stomach heaved. He thought he might vomit. But the wind forced itself into his open mouth and down his throat, diminishing the urge to gag. He threw his head back and looked at the sky; clear of clouds, smut-black and pocked with squinting stars. He barely knew who he was, where he was. The sky was above him, the water below, but that was about all that was clear.

He'd wiped his hands down over his face and walked along the path towards the jetty. A sheepdog came out of the blackness, its hair all ruffled over to one side in the wind. It sidled up, moving around Chris' legs as he walked, as if it couldn't decide which way to go. Then it fell into step beside him, its tail sweeping from side to side. When the car was a good fifty feet behind, Chris bent down, taking the dog's head in his hands, rubbing its ears and neck. Beneath its hair, the dog's skin was warm and its eyes reflected the yellow of the harbour lights. In his breast pocket, Chris felt his phone vibrate. Laura. He didn't even think not to answer. She told him to stop being ridiculous and get back in the car.

"Got to go, chum," he'd said. "Guess you should go back to your owner. I'm on my way back to mine."

There was no point in walking any further away from the car. He'd have to go back to it sometime. It was either that, or never go back at all.

When he opened the door, Laura was examining her face in the pull-down mirror.

"Let's just get home," she'd said. "We'll talk about it in the morning."

But they didn't. Sunday morning came and went. They'd done all the usual things: made the espressos, bought the papers, cooked a big breakfast. There was no need for her to elaborate. All week they went through their routine as if nothing had happened.

Now here he is, removing slugs from the plants with a zeal even he knows is suspect. Just a few more leaves to examine. He makes a third trip out to the lane, shaking out the carton, this time mostly filled with baby ones, some barely half an inch long.

Three or four have secured themselves fast to the waxy surface. He flicks them out with the twig.

He walks a few steps down the lane. The security lamp in Eddie's garden clicks on when his movement is detected, flooding the greyness with white light. Someone has been busy out here: pulling weeds, clearing the dog shit, sweeping up. A familiar red and white football sits beside a neat mound of debris. Chris picks it up, reading the name Jack Byrne scrawled over the worn surface in the child's own wobbly hand. He's held this ball before, tossing it back over Eddie's wall on countless Saturday afternoons, when father and son re-enact a Premiership game. It gives under his grip, needs pumping up.

Closing the gate behind him, Chris goes to his shed, rummages in the toolbox, pulls out the pump. Up under the heater lights, he sits, carefully fitting the needle into the tiny hole in the ball. It only takes a few seconds before it's rock hard. He thumps it onto the patio. It bounces high, coming down on the parasol, rolling off the faded fabric, hitting the ground with a smack. He moves to the one piece of open space in the garden where there are no plants, tosses the ball in the air. He heads it up, it falls, and with his flip-flopped left foot he gives it a kick. It sails at eye-level through the enclosed space, beginning its descent too near the table. He thinks about lunging forward to tap it to one side. Instead, he stands and watches as it hits its target with ease. The two crystal glasses explode, fragments skittering across the entire surface of the patio. The ball rolls off under a chair. Chris crunches over the shards to retrieve it. With a powerful underarm throw, he hurls it over the wall into Eddie's garden.

Back inside the house, he tosses the empty slug container into the recycling bin and heads up the stairs. He undresses, looks at Laura's face, her eyes too tightly shut for real sleep. He slips into the bed, careful not to touch her.

When he wakes, he's surprised he's slept at all. It's still the middle of the night. Laura is up.

"You left the lights on again. I had a feeling you would, so I went to check. Seriously Chris, how many times?"

"Sorry."

Laura throws off her dressing gown and gets back in, plumping her pillow. She lies on her side, her face turned away from her husband's.

"And our glasses are in smithereens, by the way. That cat must've been in and knocked them over. Glass everywhere. Will you sweep it up when you come home tomorrow? Don't know what time I'll get back."

"Mm, ok." He sinks further into the bed, close to sleep again.

"And I think you're going to need something more effective than your milk carton," Laura yawns, rolling the duvet in under her body. "I knew it was pointless. Patio's full of them."

Chris opens his eyes, stares into the darkness. He wants to run down to see for himself. But not yet. He waits for the signs; the erratic twitches of her limbs, the familiar rush of breath from her nose, gently swaying into the almost inaudible rhythm that signals the end of every day. Then he slips out.

He turns on the lights. She was right. Standing under the parasol, he watches them; crawling through the gap under the gate, moving across the patio like tiny flames under the orange glow. He thought he'd done such a good job. But there they are. Finding pathways back through all the bits of shattered glass.

Colin Barrett

The Dynamiters of Quebec

The duck's bill was a stubby, pumpkin orange cone, not tapering and whistle-shaped like a real duck's bill. The rest of its torso was one piece, a broad oval, with the wing, tail and breast feathers distinguished by a pattern of crude grey and green brush strokes. The duck was covered in a down of dust. Nathan ran his finger along its curved back, making a clear stripe in the fuzz that had accumulated there. The duck was part of a menagerie of porcelain waterfowl arranged on the middle shelf of the glass display cabinet in his Gran's sitting room. The lower shelf accommodated a series of china plates, each depicting a watercolour rendering of a famous historical event, and the top a row of miniature crystal timepieces, all mysteriously set at different times.

Nathan picked the porcelain duck up. It had a surprising heft and coolness to it. He splayed his fingers, as if they were wings, and rocked the duck back and forth in the air, pretending that it was flying.

Nathan wondered about things. His favourite show on TV was the one about the detective who was able to read minds, dissolve guns and flip a car up into the air with just a thought. He could tell people what they were going to do before they did it, and they did it anyway. This guy kept going on about the power of the mind. Nathan had studied diagrams of the brain in his *Puttnam's Children's Encyclopedia*, and produced his own laboriously rendered versions in the back pages of his school copybooks. He dreamed of somehow tapping into the hidden power flowing through that strange pleated mush the Encyclopedia assured him was packed in under his skull. He wondered if one day, having harnessed these powers, he would be able, for instance, to imagine this little duck into life. He pictured the duck giving a surprised, ducky honk as it realized it was alive, imagined it dazedly waddling out of his palm and setting out across the floor of his Gran's sitting room in search of some porcelain pond it would never find.

Nathan's father, Dessie Donnell, appeared in the hallway. He was a stocky man, fat in a neatly compacted way, with a full red beard, short, powerful arms and large, chunky hands, one of which was swaddled now in a mitten of inch thick gauze and surgical tape. He was scratching his beard with his other hand, his good hand. Nathan watched his father closely whenever he did this, eager to see if he would extract some hitherto concealed item from the red curls brambling his jaw line – a folded up pound note, or a hot wheels car. Nathan had given considerable thought to it and come to the conclusion that that would be the only good thing, *really*, about having a beard; that you could use it to ferry around small items, little surprises or presents. Or hang miniature baubles and streamers from it, like a Christmas tree.

Dessie came into the sitting room and looked down at his son, noticing the object half concealed in Nathan's hand. "What are you at, Nathy?" he hissed, "*please* don't break anything!"

Nathan followed his dad's eyes down to his hand. The porcelain duck squatted in his palm like something incriminating.

"Nothing, I'm not doing *anything*," he said, quickly replacing the duck on the glass shelf. And this was true. Nathan had been up to absolutely nothing, but still, he felt his face flush, the admonitory note in his father's voice enough to make him feel implicated – in what, he couldn't say, but whatever it was it had not eluded Dessie's attention.

Dessie ceased scratching at his beard and placed his good hand on his hip and sighed. He moved over to the window. As he breathed in and out, his head, shoulders and chest moved up and down together in arduous sync. Nathan watched his dad turn his bandaged hand in the air, very slowly, the muscles in his thick arm tensing with the effort. He'd burned it a week ago, hosting a backyard barbeque for the dynamiters from Quebec. From his position on the floor, Nathan could not see out the window but knew it was raining, in the way you know these things without having to check. Nathan's mum, Soosie, had flown back to the States three days ago, to visit her sister, Amy, who was sick in some serious, unspecified way, and it seemed to Nathan that his father had been in a bad mood since.

He was going to ask Dessie to tell him a football story, thinking that this might help lift him out of his funk. But it seemed to Nathan that he had heard them all a bazillion times, the football stories, and a part of him understood that his father didn't really like talking about that stuff anyway.

Back in the day, Dessie Donnell had been something of a sporting prodigy. As a young man in the late '70s, he'd played Gaelic football for Mayo before progressing into professional league football in England. He'd played centre midfield for West Brom and Wolves, and at twenty five had moved to the US, where he'd turned out for the New York Cosmos in the glitzy North American Soccer League, briefly lining up in the same team as an aging Franz Beckenbauer. It was in the States that he'd met Nathan's mother. Soosie was an NASL cheer leader, an Irish American out of Boston. Her maiden name was Reilly.

Nathan had seen the faded newsprint pictures, the full colour action snaps and laminated team photos: his father, unnaturally trim, in straining '80s shorts and hair. Reassuringly, he'd had a beard even then.

Dessie's football career ended in the autumn of '83; three games into that league season he'd blown his knee out, irreparably. Nathan was born not long after, by which time Dessie, still in a cast and support brace, had just about managed to hobble down the aisle with Soosie. The following year the NASL folded forever and Dessie, new family in tow, had come back across the Atlantic, back to Mayo.

After a moment Nathan, aware of a silence that seemed housewide, changed tack and asked, "where's Gran?"

Dessie sucked in his teeth, evidently aggravated by the question, even though it was an entirely reasonable one, as far as Nathan could see. They'd pulled up here, at his Gran's house, over half an hour ago. Nathan had been escorted to the sitting room and told to stay put while Dad and his Gran had removed themselves to the kitchen to talk their grownup talk.

Nathan was getting hungry. Dessie had insisted they skip breakfast, which Nathan hadn't minded as Dessie had also informed him he would not be going to school today either, although he had waited until *after* Nathan had put on his school uniform to tell him that. Hence Nathan, stretched out on the carpet of his Gran's sitting room, in the grey slacks, pale blue shirt and navy jumper of his uniform. He had already removed his tie and balled it into his pocket, and with his fingers he now began to tease out the loose thread of his jumper's fraying left sleeve, in blatant violation of his mother's repeated entreaties. Despite the curt dismissals of his father, Nathan really did feel as if he should, after all, be in school today.

"Gran's on the phone, Nate," Dessie said, trying to sound as casual as he could. He reached for the curtains and grabbed a fistful of faded white lace in his good hand. He held it up close to his face.

"Fucking filthy," he muttered under his breath, flicking the lumpy apostrophe of a dead fly off the curtain.

"Who's she talking to?"

Dessie sighed, then admitted, "Mam, actually."

"Mam?"

"Yep."

Nathan thought about this – was she ringing to say she was coming back, or had there been a delay of some sort?

The night before Soosie left, his parents had argued. Nathan had been watching TV in the sitting room. His parents' raised voices had come through the wall with a muffled, submerged quality, as if they were trying to fight their way out of some great depth. Nathan had to concentrate hard to keep his attention fixed inside the bright perimeter of the TV as they went at it. They were in the kitchen. His parents were always careful never to fight directly in front of Nathan, and he knew that if he were to walk in right then, they would have stopped dead. This was, Nathan supposed, an attempt to protect him, but it only succeeded in making Nathan feel weirdly culpable – as if, despite all evidence to the contrary, it was *him* they were always fighting about. Dessie and Soosie had all sorts of useless rules like that – like all the worst wars, their fights were governed by a series of elaborate proscriptions and observances that served only to exacerbate, or make more apparent, the very things they were intended to hide or diminish.

On the TV the wrestler Ric Flair, veins bulging like tree roots under his skin, was shouting down a crowd, his bested opponent doddering like a blind man around the ring. As usual, Nathan wasn't sure who had started the fight.

The next morning, a Saturday, rain had ticked against the bedroom windows like the scuttling of some enormous, many legged insect. Nathan came up out of a dream to find a skinny pterodactyl perched at the end of his bed. As he rubbed his eyes and yawned, the pterodactyl resolved itself into the lean, angular figure of his mother. She was talking, and by the time Nathan started listening she had already nearly finished explaining how very unexpected it had been but that she had to go back to the States, right that morning, that something very important had happened with her sister, and that she had to go see her straight away, but that she would be back very, very soon. She'd swooped down and kissed him just under his right eye. Nathan had squished his face back into his pillow and let out an appalled grunt. Soosie had put her hands on his shoulders and just sat there, saying nothing. Determined to fall back asleep, Nathan kept his eyelids screwed tight, the wingtips of his nostrils flaring minutely and evenly in a brutal approximation of what he felt resembled a state of composed unconsciousness. Moments passed; he didn't notice the deft subtraction of his mother's hands from his shoulders, didn't notice her stand up, waver, shut the door. By the time she left the room, he had fallen back to sleep for real.

That was three days ago. But she would be back soon. He knew she would be back soon, but for now she was gone and her absence was something Nathan was attempting to ignore and, at the same time, get used to. It didn't help that the Donnell household, left in the charge of father and son, had descended into a state of chaos. A landslide of encrusted crockery had buried the sink and draining board. The kitchen's lino flooring alternately crunched and squelched stickily underfoot. In the bathroom, a halo of congealed soapscum ringed the inside of the white tub, and an engorged and apparently inextricable slub of sodden red hair squatted in the sinkhole, shivering malevolently whenever a swirl of water ran through it. Nathan's duvet and bed pillows had become bunched and twisted into a single cloudlike mass that remained lumpily impervious to any attempt to bludgeon it back into its original components, and a reek of burnt toast lingered stubbornly in the air.

As his mother's stand-ins, Nathan and his father were a halting and cumbersome two man team, allocating household duties as they discovered them, seeking only to temporize and contain. But they were failing. Nathan had been assigned a series of routine tasks – changing the kitchen bin bags, restocking the pail of fireside briquettes, but found these chores maddeningly repetitive and tedious. Nathan was lazy. What his mother did, running their lives – it was work, Nathan understood. She braided up all their loose ends and smoothed out all their edges. And in her absence his father seemed as lost as him.

"*Dad,*" he said finally, "what are we doing here? What's *happening*?"

Dessie grinned wanly and shook his head.

"Jesus, Nathy. If I knew that."

Gran's bedroom door shunted open at the end of the hall. Lenora Donnell, stooped and walking with a determined turtle gait, inched out of her bedroom and came towards her son and grandson. She was seventy two, a farmer's widow, and was dressed, as usual, in a man's white polo vest, wool cardigan, Wellington boots and a tablecloth-like red and white gingham skirt. Her one concession to ornament was the tarnished silver locket she wore around her neck, which contained a tiny, near obliterated black and white portrait of her own grandmother. The skin of her face was like a sheet of paper that had been scrunched up and flattened back out again, and her hair, a blue-rinse bouffant, resembled a tuft of decrepit cotton candy.

"Des....Des" she raised her hand toward Dessie, "talk to her. Talk to her. Come on, talk to her."

Gran kept the only phone in her house by her bedside; an old fashioned rotary model with a big receiver, it crouched inert on her wardrobe tabletop like a many eyed and shiny black crustacean.

"*I'll* talk to her," Nathan offered.

"Just stay there," Dessie growled at Nathan. He moved past his mother and down the hallway and went into his mother's room. Nathan heard the door shut.

His Gran looked at Nathan, who had drawn his knees up under his chin, fetal against the foot of the pillow festooned couch. After a moment of silence, she said, "how's that eejit's hand Nathy, does he say much about it giving him trouble?"

"I don't know," Nathan said truthfully.

Nathan went outside. The rain had stopped, and there was a ringing stillness like after you wrench open a drawer of cutlery. He liked the sucky noises the dirt made when he pressed his shoes into it and pulled them away.

He'd asked his Gran if she'd anything to eat and admitted that he and his father had skipped breakfast. Gran had tutted and said she'd fix something for him and headed off toward the kitchen. Nathan had thought about what to do next, and, when he couldn't think of anything, decided to go outside for a wander. After that, he'd picked his way quietly past his Gran's room, his father's voice coming faintly through the door. The door was wooden, painted white, with tiny hardened blobs in it where the paint had trapped an air bubble and blistered. Nathan could trace with his fingers the thumbprint-intricate lines and spirals of the door's grain, faintly visible beneath the applied layers of white. Nathan had thought about pressing his ear to the keyhole, or crouching down to the dusty slice of space between the bottom of the door and the saddle, but decided to keep going. He'd been warned about eavesdropping, and was fearful of doing it just then, the urge to listen competing with the fear of overhearing precisely the thing tempting him to consider eavesdropping in the first place. So he went by the door and turned left into the kitchen. He waved "hi" to his Gran, busy uncanning beans into a metal saucepan, and opened the back door. He hopped the low, whitewashed stone wall that enclosed the back yard. There was a neglected flower patch in one corner of the garden, next to a pile of turf covered by a length of flapping black tarp, which if you watched long enough, Nathan knew, would begin to flap in a way that eventually came to seem deliberate, as if it were attempting to impart a message. There was an old tractor too, his dead Grandda's '72 Massey that had, by now, fossilised into a piece of junkyard sculpture, spider webs glimmering in the spaces up under the wheels, braids of ancient, discoloured dirt lining the tyre ruts. Everything else was just swathes and humps of grass, yellowing and rampantly overgrown. The blade tips came up to his navel. A couple of Gran's cats slithered silently through it, slick with wetness. They moved fluently, fur shining, whiskers ticking; Nathan half expected them to leave dark streaks in their wake. And then the sun was in his eyes, like a veil made of light.

His parents had thrown the barbeque a week ago. Dessie had invited over his newest work buddies, the Quebec dynamiters; Quebec was a place in Canada where people talked French and cultivated the inborn urge to blow stuff up toward socially productive ends. The Quebeckers worked for Nathan's father, and Dessie worked for the Electricity Supply Board. Dessie and the Quebeckers had spent the last three months working in Connemara, up in the Twelve Bens Mountains. It was there that the site for a new hydro electric power station was being developed. Hydro-electric, Nathan knew, meant the generation of electricity from water and the really interesting thing was that the station was going to be built *inside* one of the mountains. This is why the demolition team had been brought in; they'd to blow out the myriad tunnels and spaces in the mountain in which the various parts of the electrical station were to be built and housed. When his father had explained it to him one evening, Nathan had envisaged a sprawling, super villain-like lair of futuristic equipment embedded in a series of stadium sized subterranean cavities, the entire mountain awash in squalls, cataracts and riverine crackles of blue electric light. Dessie promised Nathan he would take him up there to have a look when it was finished.

There were five Quebeckers at the barbeque, to a man, as beefy and hairy as Nathan's father. They had flowery French sounding names – Francois, Pierre, Stephan – that melted together in Nathan's head. They shouted at each other and laughed with their whole bodies and their laughter actually sounded like detonations going off in their chests. When they talked, their English lapsed into French and then back again, and their hands were going the whole time, looping and fluttering. They'd snagged a couple of local girls and brought them along. One of them, wearing a check shirt and a bright orange hockey cap, creaked a deck chair and bounced a girl a third his size on his knee. The bill of the cap shaded the upper half of his face and reduced his eyes to two tiny, moist points of light. He pursed his lips and called the girl his *baayy beee*, his fingers hopscotching along the notches of her spine.

"Zoozie," he'd roared, "Zoozie, come and meet Gryawn-ya, you knowzis girl?"

That was the weird thing about this particular Quebecker; he kept dragging over Nathan's mother to talk to the girl – Gráinne – he was with, like she was supposed to be impressed or something. His mother just flicked her eyes and blew at her fringe, and it was also annoying the girl, who wriggled up off the Quebecker's lap and went to get another beer. His mother was great at these parties, Nathan thought. She wandered in and out of groups and conversations, smiling and laughing, like she was old friends with everybody, even though she didn't know any of them.

There'd been a lot of drinking. Nathan loped on the periphery of things, scavenging cold chips from abandoned paper plates and helping himself to long gaseous chugs from the two-litre bottles of store brand Coke laid out with all the beer. As the sky went blue and pink, midges began to fizz in the air and braid tiny fires into Nathan's scalp. And then the accident had happened. Someone – a girl, maybe Gráinne – had let out a high pitched screech and Nathan had turned to see his father bent double, clutching his hand, gone bright pink, by the wrist. A wisp of smoke came up off his skin and flapped away, like a butterfly. The barbeque stand had been tipped over, hunks of coal and blackened meat smoking in the grass. When Nathan heard his father let out that first, startlingly alien roar of pain, he did what any boy would do – he looked for the face of his mother. And there she was. To Nathan's surprise she was standing beside the Quebecker in the deck chair. The Quebecker's hand – thick and meaty just like Nathan's father's – floated in the air up by her side. The tips of his fingers, no doubt as callus riddled as Dessie's, were just touching Soosie's wrist, and as Dessie let out another growl of pain Nathan watched as his mother's fingers opened and then closed tightly around the Quebecker's hand.

Look at the sun too long and it will turn your eyes to cinders. Nathan lowered his head and squatted low in the back yard grass. If he leaned forward, down onto his chest, he was almost completely invisible, he was sure, to any and all potential observers. His father waddled out of the house, looking this way and that as he tramped as far as the parked Corolla and then over to the whitewashed wall. He stopped there, his gut resting on the lip of the wall, and shouted out, "Nate!"
He shouted again.
"Nathan!"
Nathan stretched out and pressed himself further into the grass. He was on his belly, and could no longer see his father, or his Gran's house, just the incline of the slate roof, blackboard black and glistening in the drenched sunlight. He thought, with a measure of satisfaction, about how perplexed and miserably stupid his father must be feeling right now, having gone and lost his only son in the back yard of his own childhood home. As his father let out another, longer yell, now properly shot through with anger, Nathan caught and stifled with a forceful gulp the thing welling in his throat, and pressed his forehead into the wet soil. The dark earth pressed right up against his eyes. He thought about the porcelain duck on the glass shelf and how wrong it would be, if he had the power, to bring the duck to life; it was better off the way it was, in its appointed spot on the middle shelf of the glass cabinet, time passing over and around it with the harmlessness of weather observed through a window. The darkness was such that Nathan could no longer tell if his eyes were open or closed, but he knew he could stay like this, easily, for the next hour, the day, possibly forever.

John Taylor

Belfast *Flâneur*

I

Rye smells rise from a concrete speckled in damp stubs
Towards sandstone window frames, filled glassy green, all
Figure and crucifixions, here, by St. Anne's, where I cross the road
Cupped in the warm rush of traffic and the spring fall.

Loiter on the curb, let the people pass and dwell in reflections.
God's behind me at least a while, only footsteps make a sound today.
Past flavoured Duke of York, Donegall Street's paint needs a touch,
In dirt and shaded spots, I trip over the history that's made in alleyways.

A host of hooting sirens at the lights, I catch the tail of chats,
Of couples sitting and kids pirouetting, once sobered on Royal Avenue.
All clamour and demand now, sweltering in the soggy morning sun,
The roll call of shops rolls out, perfectly stuffed, ready to be passed through.

I get my paper out by the trees of City Hall, the bench and page today
Scored in names and lines and hearts and who knows what they'll all bloody say.

III

From her house, after duelling the double lanes,
I walked down a Georgian clay row: with its cracks
The grey slates held up the houses. I collapsed,
Accepting tiredness after play, in a time-full retreat:

A season of cherry in the trees and the chance
Of long lie-ins along Botanic Garden's banks,
No Ball Games but couples nonetheless
Kissing, reading or lazily passing to the Museum.

The dazzles of yellow cups threw their scent over
The green, flattened and fresh and seeing out the morning ...

Snug city nest, independent of the rush
Of what is coming or from that old presence –
That lurk of shadow in an open stretch; well, it can watch,
We're the audience and the act with our senses now playing too.

V

Reid's Shoes, Sandy Row (where years back a
Purple-tuft toy clown twirled in the window
Around a pole) faces the snub of Dublin and Great
Victoria Street; furrow fares together. Here, bricks pattern
The side and path, a stream of litter lifts in a quick gust,
The doorsteps and fronts show a perpetuity-ness forwards
To Bedford with the waver of reflections … I wonder if I

Can change mid stride? The sombre Fountain Bar smirks
Around its corner pushing the city's minglers about,
Governed alone by the hand that holds their own, braced
In a brawl accent and the weekend's game, but each
Undoubtedly awake. Dutifully I'll wait and see:
Nearby grim smoke-fused faces, framed in brown and white,
Stare out and out from the docks, decades ago, unendingly.

By the Waterfront

The rain still crests sloppily, hanging hazily through
The brace of cold that succumbs the Northerner,
Standing now by polished cocoons whose
Windows still reflect the lurid water wrinkles

Of the gently curving Lagan; a body rapt in
Familiar thoughts, breadth still forging our way.
This is the new quarter shadowed
In glassy cathedrals, balconies and odd droplets of sun

Where the powder-like yellow stone gleams.
Yet still the whipper-snapper wind pants
Through red bricked market stalls and vacant fish,
Through drinks and theatre winks in evening dress.

For at night the lights dazzle that water top –
Flaking greens kiss the timid hues before the brave
Starriness guides each waver below the bridge –
David and Goliath sneak in if you've got a 'postcard' eye

While a woman performs her statuesque duty
Standing upon the world, no Atlas beneath,
Yet still the Northerner cries the same:
Roundly ready for a creamy head, a bit of banter

In the queue, a decent measure in the tank.
Spawn in a murky pool, but un-expectantly open
To the new smell of a wet body, to flush lights,
Even if they'll all forget him on his journey home.

Night Guard

I can see you as if once a night guard
Pacing the vacantly lit aisles of a store.

You are dressed appropriately:
Starched shirt, obedient tie, a badge

Above a baton that never swings.
A dedication for a life.

The silence doesn't disturb
The check for lurking shadows,

For any irregular door locks
Before the sleeping products

Dreaming in the silent air
The cold licking the store room door.

The Bonfires

Tomorrow's colours are given a fourth tonight.
Jobless young men have jobs the past fortnight.
Scavenging for crates, creating the space.
Corners of communities mounted together,

incongruously in the stack. In the blaze.
You can feel the heat lengths back.
When the green flag goes up, tribal roars erupt,
it's a wonder what century it is.

Lagan Bridge

I

The River Farset, shouldering the silky
blackness of sand and mud,
cogging together, stilling
under the High Street footsteps,

blends towards the new powerhouses.

II

The brown overcoat of
Lagan water nudges its own
bank side becoming cupped clear
in hands;
the boats drift together
and let their paint chip and drop

into the dark wet-rung tufts.
Daily, the Weir labours over
the river turnover; a muscle
now from a Slieve Croob stream.

III

Follow the walkway past clay estates
where tree branches
clasp and crawl across the surface.

Beyond leafy Queens now, the bridge
is high to a low lying frame.
Inquisitiveness possesses
the crosser

to dip under the lapping
wrapping wavelets
or to simply hover,
if the smell permits,
above the watermark.

IV

The breeze picks up on this vaulted point
overcasting the stretching summer-night-yellows
thrown off Cutters pub.

It winds its way through the railings
where I passed her,

imagining her: eyes full of pity
ignited beneath the lamplight
as the Lagan crept on to stray,

her hand down my front
tugging pasts away.

Dublin Strand

Where the twin towers with red and white rims
stand abrupt before a flat edge
the swarming smoke signals

upon this open fortress
goalposts for the Gods
and for the match to begin ...

Divots in sand plied with
pebble or grain squelch
of a lengthy time before
as it rises, form mightily unbound,

a silvery blue. Arms immaculately shake,
legs too percolate
the sea to petulant waves;
the glassy water silks around
the marauding figure
embraced in spray and rival

formations. It weaves those weaker
nymphs under a watery spell
and kicks for goal ... the crowded
sky goes wild.

And after, this God of lurid stadiums
tames, flattening its spirit within
the surface justified

that drifting walkers
and weary front bench spectators
with Sunday sandwiches
should rightly marvel.

Migration at UCD

It will be autumn soon and coloured
leaves will drift back to the ground.

I watch you from my Friday afternoon window
walking in proudly diagonal fashions
across the green.

A popular chorus
with pink weekend suitcases –
aren't you so hip! or hilarious? – flocking
to the fold.
Back to the familiar pillows, back to the garden
seat and grandfather's kettle.

In what looks like numbness I sit
tapestried in freshly woven friends,
their words spring like sling shots across
burnished land rupturing
once hardened walls,

and when the dust settles I know
gentle workings brooding
in time ignite next year's branches.

Anne Graham

Jesus Christ Pose

The river flows. And he with it. Why he always comes here he never knows. Its thickness pulls him under. Here, there is no sound, no movement, like the hushed aftermath of a great speech or the clean silence after a gun has been fired. That clear instant where neither morals nor evil matter. It just is. But then, as always, the river gets cold and nips at his skin. The anxiety returns; his peace never lasting long. Usually, he never goes too far downriver and makes his way back up the rapids easily enough. But this time, the current has different ideas. It sweeps him away, as a hand sweeps crumbs off a table.

He wakes to find himself on the riverbank. Where is he? Moss surrounds him like an armchair. But he is not comfortable. After clambering up the bank, he finds himself facing a forest. It is not the whimsical forest of Bambi. It is dense and imposing. The trees are bullish looking, with muscular, ribbed trunks. The branches sway like sabres. He has to get home. He turns a hundred and eighty degrees, intending to return to the river bank and walk along it until he reaches calmer waters. But the river is no longer there. The forest must have decided to cover up its embarrassing leak. Now he is surrounded by thickness. He hears whispers, sharp hisses like a snake being stepped on. The branches crackle as if flexing their muscles. He has to get out of here. There must be a path somewhere.

He staggers through the mounds of dark grass. They look like hairy bubonic boils. Unnerved, he decides to look straight ahead and hope for the best. This plan is decidedly flawed. Unsurprisingly, he trips over one of the mounds and falls face down. His eyes soon find the reason why the grass is so black. Thousands of microscopic snails slide across it, leaving an oily stain. It stinks of decay, and oddly, a bit like shortbread. He thinks of his great-grandmother who always gave the family those biscuits for Christmas. She died in her bed in a nursing home. He feels his innards erupt in protest. He drags himself up. He gasps. *What is going on here? I don't remember seeing this.* The unpredictable forest has performed one of its tricks again. A large field seems to have shouldered the trees out to its edges. It is full of roses. Black roses. He has never seen nor heard of a black rose. Possibly the work of those horrible snails. He groans. He will have to go through the field to get to the forest on the other side. The thought of the thorns pricking him makes him shudder. But he has to get home. As he wades through this black sea, he draws a sigh of relief; luckily, his jeans seem to ward off most of the impact. He looks up at the sky. He isn't very sure if he could call it a sky. It is all white. There are no variations, no gradations of colour or clouds. Just pure white. He feels awed and daunted by it.

As he is staring at this, he hears a giggle like soft chimes blowing in the wind. He looks around. Behind him is a little girl. She must be about seven, he can't really tell as he's never been good at guessing ages. Her waist-length hair is colourless and blends in with the sky above. She wears what looks to him to be a white communion dress with a black ribbon around the waist and black buckle shoes. Her faint lips smile at him strangely, expectantly. There is a knowing, almost comical look in her eyes. In her hand she holds one of the black roses.

"Here you are, I picked this especially for you. It's your favourite."

Without meaning to be rude, he just stands there in puzzlement. "How can it be my favourite when I've never even seen one before?"

A haughty laugh. "Don't be silly. It's always been your favourite. You created it, after all."

"No I didn't," he says with surprise. "Did I?"

She begins laughing her chime laugh but as she goes on, it deepens to an organ timbre. She is no longer a little girl but a fully grown woman. He must have blinked and somehow missed the transformation. In her mature incarnation, she has a black dress with a white ribbon around the waist. She wears no shoes. Her hair has turned black and is as slick as the oil from the snails. The face is still the same but the eyes are now burning with vice and loathing. Their hungry look seems voracious yet empty somehow, like there is no point to it.

"Take it, take it!" She snarls at him as she tries to thrust the rose into his hand. "It's your favourite." She screams mockingly. "It won't hurt that much, Sleeping Beauty." The thorns already feel like they are gnawing at him like piranhas.

He runs. He runs and he doesn't look back. He couldn't bear looking at that face again. He wills the trees on the other side to reach out their spindly arms and grab him to safety. His wish is granted. In a round about way. He is on the ground before he realises what is happening. The roots encircling his limbs like twine. He looks like a human ball of wool. His cry of terror has no echo. No one is going to answer him back. He finds himself being drawn in the direction of a huge tree. All the smaller trees seem to gather round it at a respectful distance, their limbs bent over in prostration. The big tree lifts its roots up like multiple stringy tongues, allowing the dark underbelly to swallow him up.

It is pitch black but he can tell he is sitting in a chair. It is that precarious kind of chair whose legs are weak, uncertain. He doubts that they will support his weight. Before he has a chance to move, he hears a clink. A light directly overhead showers him with its intensity. He feels naked. Then all of a sudden, a desk jumps out of nowhere before him with what appears to be a textbook upon it. Another light switches on. He finds himself before a man. The man looks normal enough with a pristine, well-pressed shirt tucked inside neat slacks and a 1950s crew cut. But he doesn't *feel* normal. There is something definitely menacing about him. The light seems to accentuate certain parts of his face, with the result that it looks like a fierce cliff. He has a long bamboo cane in his hand.

"Well? What's the answer?" he asks impatiently.

"I, I haven't even read the question, sir." The Pupil feels compelled to add the authoritative title.

"Read it? You don't read it, you're supposed to know, don't you know that? But of course not, it is you after all." He lashes the cane over the Pupil's hands. A high-pitched yelp is the reply.

"I must concede, you are good at something. At being stupid. Grade A student, I must say. But I digress."

He claps his hands and several more lights switch on. They are no longer alone. A group of roughly ten young men dressed exactly the same as the Teacher, crowd around the desk. Their plastered smiles are disturbing crescents. They all wear silver medals around their necks which shine brightly, tackily.

"And now for the presentation," the Teacher trumpets. One of the men hands him a small box. The Teacher takes out a medal exactly the same as the others. He puts it around the Pupil's neck. He gasps at the weight of it. It is so heavy that he is stooped over, his chin touching his chest. All the men laugh uproariously, interjecting snorts like pigs.

The Teacher sneers. "Just as I expected. Can't bear the weight. Don't look down, you might fall!"

They all laugh again and someone pushes him onto the floor. "Come on now, old dog," he feels the sting of the cane on his back, "let's have a little parade!"

All he can see is the ground, as he crawls along, sometimes coerced by a foot or the cane. It looks like TV static. Endless, endless. The blurred aspect of it makes him so dizzy, that he soon passes out.

He awakes to find himself in a completely different setting: lying on many layers of rich Persian rugs. He is nearly blinded by the gaudiness. The reds in particular give him a headache. He hears a shuffle behind a Japanese screen. It reminds him of an attention-seeking cough. Out walks the most horribly beautiful woman he has ever seen. Everything about her follows da Vinci's rules of proportion but he cannot help feeling a sense of revulsion. Like the rugs, her features are too extravagant. Her eyes big and blue, heavily adorned by rapier-like lashes. Her nose small, lit with an insincere sheen. Her hair is eye-dissolving gold. It goes down to her knees; too weighty a treasure. Her lips are big and sensuous, ready to engulf even with the slightest parting. She is perfect. Perfectly awful. She does not appear to notice him. She is engrossed in a mirror she holds up to her face. Its angular reflections fit into the angles of her face like jigsaw pieces. She is so wrapped up in her gazing that she trips up over the edge of a rug. She lands in a mess of silks and underclothing. The mirror has fallen beside him. He picks it up intending to return it to its owner. He happens to spy his image in it. It shatters completely; no glass remains.

"Oh pah, pah, look what you've done. Your face, too ugly in the way it moves. Too animated." She says this with complete disgust. "Oh well, luckily I have spare." Her lips are like smug sausages. She takes an even bigger mirror out of a drawer. She seats herself on a chaise longue sighing with delight. "Perfection," she whispers. Something glints beneath her seat. Eyes. Big eyes, staring at him constantly, without blinking.

"Sorry for interrupting your eh...you...but there's something underneath your seat. And it keeps staring at me."

She exhales with exasperation. "Oh for heaven's sake, it's not staring at you. It's just staring in general. Always so quick to assume."

He is about to reply when he hears a shout coming from the other side of a door beside the chaise longue. It sounds amplified. A microphone? It booms like a series of sombre explosions.

"Oh for...why do they always want to interrupt me? Can't they see it's important? Of the utmost importance. Go tell them to stop." She says all this without looking away from the mirror. He is glad to leave her and her nauseating opulence.

He opens the door and finds himself in a small theatre. The seats look brand new, a shiny red. Upon the mahogany stage is the source of the commotion. His favourite Comedian! The tickets for the last series of shows had sold out before he could get one. But now he has the pick of the seats and the show all to himself. He seats himself in the front row, the aisle seat, dead centre. The spectator shifts around in excitement. But it soon turns to sinking dread as he tunes into the Comedian's words. Gone are the trademark surrealist rants that express subtly what most of us are afraid to say on certain, everyday topics. Instead – "The chicken walked to the other side of the road and said "amn't I great", ha ha! And so did the tortoise and he felt even better because he was really slow about it. But since cars weren't invented at that time, around 20,000 BC, he was safe. But then why did they have roads? Oh for chickens and tortoises to cross of course ha ha! But wait, why would they want to cross the road? Chickens and tortoises don't strike me as adventurous types really ha!" The Comedian looks lost. His eyes are squinting under the scrutiny of the stage lights. He then spots the Spectator.

"You! You have ruined me. Before you came along I was Comedy Gold. Now I'm Comedy Old." The Spectator is too shocked at his hero's admonishment of him to react.

"And my juice. Yes my life-blood. My accomplice, comrade-in-arms won't come out of his room because of you. Look."

A screen at the back of the stage lifts, revealing a row of doors. The door in the middle is illuminated more than the others. It has the compulsory star on it. Emblazoned upon it is the name 'Mirr, Hugh'.

"Yes! Yes that's right!" The comedian shouts in that famous jerky manner of his. "Ruined. Ruined it all. Happy are you? No, never!" He shakes his head violently, his lank locks now pointing to the ceiling in a surprised manner. He starts ranting incoherently, kicking at invisible objects of hatred. A few minutes later he jerks to a sudden stop.

"Security! Get him out of my sight. No more."

Two imposing marble statues with Romanesque features grab each of his arms which are nearly crushed. They throw him against the wall several times in an alternating game of squash. Finally, they open a steel door that is embedded in the plaster walls that are now decorated with artistic flourishes of his blood. They throw him through it, the closing door sounding like a shouting giant. It takes him a long time to get off the floor. When he does, he gradually realises he is in a chapel. It is dimly lit by a few battered candelabras; they feebly try to cast their dull flickers over the domineering shadows. The whole place has a sense of decrepitude about it. The floor is disturbed by gaps that have bitten away at the mosaic patterns. The walls possess remains of murals; the colours seem to have rebelled against the rules of Classicism and bled into each other. Now all that remains is a sickly mish-mash. The seats, or what's left of them, are slanted diagonally. It gives the impression of an arrow on a runway. It is pointing towards the altar. Upon it is an imposing sight. A cross. A cross, with someone on it. He limps as fast as he can towards it. As he comes closer to the figure, he cries out audibly. It is *him*! Up there on the cross.

"What am I doing, I mean, what are you doing up there?" He is at a loss.

"Save me," is the raspy reply.

"Save you?" He doesn't seem to understand the words. As he looks on in desperate confusion, a thought gives him a sharp nudge. "But aren't you supposed to save me? Isn't that the point? To cleanse me?"

The figure on the cross starts to weep. Tears slide down the blood matted face. It whispers breathlessly. "Please save me, I don't want to be up here anymore."

"No and I don't want you to be either." He runs up to the cross and tries to pull the nails out of the feet. They won't budge. The blood gleams at him angrily. He keeps trying for a long time but there is nothing he can do. He falls to his knees in exhaustion. He looks up. The bloodied form doesn't seem to be moving. "No! Please! You can't! I wanted to save you! I tried, I TRIED!" He hugs the feet tightly and kisses them with his tear-stained mouth. His body aches with pain. He cannot let go. Suddenly, he hears a creak, so small that he wonders how he heard it. "Over there," a voice whispers.

The door of what he assumes is the vestry is framed by a confident but not brilliant light. It is not intimidated by the darkness of the chapel. He approaches it with trepidation, inhales to full lung capacity and opens the door. It does not take his eyes long to adjust to the outside light as it is quite dull. The feel of the sand under his feet is hard but not uncomfortable. The sea is calm, the waves lapping the shore in a conciliatory manner. He feels calm. He strokes the water cautiously. It is quite warm. As he stares at all before him, he hears a muffled sound, seemingly from above him. He looks up at the sky, which is the colour of dirty bathwater. And then…a giant head appears over the horizon. It seems to be a woman but he cannot be sure, her features are so large that it is hard to focus on them. Then, with a flash, she disappears, and the sky is a dull tone again. His heart is racing. But not with fear. He looks at the sea again and smiles. Then another flash of white….

The sterile white of the ceiling comes into view. He is lying in a bed. The woman appears again. His mother. Tears slide down her face, which is contorted in a confused state of relief and questioning dismay. He feels her hand holding his. It is warm.

That night he lies there with the tubes, drips and charts surrounding him. He does not notice them. All he can hear are the gentle waves moving back and forth.

Anne Coughlan

To Hell with Poverty, Let's Kill a Chicken

A Memoir of the 1960s

As the rickety old double-decker bus trundled into town, my sister and I felt increasingly nauseous. Even though the journey only took about forty minutes, the combination of excitement, engine fumes and the rattling of the bus over bumpy streets, made it feel like an eternity. The low sun shining through the grimy bus windows didn't help. To avoid being sick, we got off the bus at Donnybrook, two-thirds of the way into town. This wasn't unusual for my sister and me. Not having a car, we would feel sick within five minutes of getting into any vehicle. It was always a question of how long we could hold on. We were relieved to get off the bus and feel the cool, fresh air and the steady ground under our feet. We did feel guilty though, for the trouble we were causing and to make sure our mother knew how necessary it had been for us to get off the bus, we gulped at the air as if our lives depended on it. As was generally the case, within a few minutes we had recovered and pronounced ourselves ready to carry on with our adventure.

And it was an adventure. Just that morning, right after our father left for work, my mother made an announcement to my sister and me.

"Put away your schoolbags, girls", she said, "you're not going to school today. We are all going into town." She was smiling. "We," and she waited, "are going shopping." Again she waited, looking at us expectantly. My sister and I looked at each other.

"What?" we asked. We didn't understand. What did 'going shopping' mean? We could feel the hint of promise in what she was saying but we were scared to ask, to test it out, in case it disappeared. I was swiftly running through my mind to see what the pitfalls might be. Then I remembered.

"Irish dancing competition – today – in school – we can't go into town." I said.

"Sure, you're always having dancing competitions in school," she said, "you won't be missed this once." That was partly true, there had been a few competitions during the year, but we weren't *always* having them. I wasn't sure that I wanted to miss this competition. The 'shopping' thing, well, I just wasn't sure what the 'shopping' thing actually was, and so I still hesitated.

"Clothes, dresses," she said loudly, slightly exasperated, "and maybe a tennis racquet." And slowly the penny dropped. We let what she was saying a little into our bones and shook it about a bit. The world flipped slightly into a brighter place. She wanted to bring us into town to buy something for us. This would mean no school. No sitting quietly and stiffly at our desks staring out the window or at the classroom clock. And what would we buy? We were going into town. We smiled back at her and I didn't ask the question that was jumping up and down in my mind – where would we get the money from?

We looked up the bus timetable and set off down the road. I was embarrassed to be seen walking down the road with my mother and sister at a time when I should have been at school. I was afraid someone might ask us where we were going. What would we say? Surely not something as extravagant as 'going shopping' on a school day? I kept my eyes on the ground. I didn't want anyone to see my excitement, or my mother's either. And yet I was a little disappointed that we didn't meet anyone. The roads were surprisingly empty.

"Town, please," my mother said to the bus conductor, "one and two halves," and he rolled off the tickets from his machine. There weren't many passengers on the bus. We watched silently as my mother chatted to the conductor. She wasn't sad. She laughed a lot more than at home. She and the conductor found common ground in a discussion about west of Ireland people being the best people, and how you would always know them, even in the city. "You're right there Missus, there is nothing like west of Ireland people." I looked out the window and wondered if I could spot them. We reached the terminus. The conductor helped us down off the bus. "Good day now, Missus and God bless yous."

At one point while we were on the bus, I'd wondered where my mother got the money to go to town. I discovered at some later stage in my life, that my mother had borrowed a hundred pounds from her friend, Mrs O'Brien. Now it's hard to say exactly how much that was worth back in the early '60s, but it would have been in the region of one thousand euros or more now. I wonder if my mother thought at all about how she was going to pay it back. My father, with his civil service job, was unlikely to ever come up with that kind of spare money and there would have been other priorities for it if he had. I also wondered if my father knew where we were that day. He would have been furious, but I quickly pushed that thought out of my mind.

My mother's reputation of having been a little wild when she was young, sat in the background of our lives. She spoke as if she could have taken on any challenge, done anything. "I could have run this country," she used to say. There was a lot of talk about dancing. She used to tell us about how she got pneumonia one time, having cycled from Dublin to Arklow. She danced for two nights and proceeded to cycle home in the rain, to get back in time for work the next day. She was not at all put out about the wetting she got. She talked about her pneumonia as if it were a medal or a badge of honour she'd got for dancing. She certainly let us know how much she enjoyed dancing. She came more alive when she talked about it – eyes shining, hands moving and her head tossed back and never missed an opportunity to demonstrate her skill when music came on the radio. We all knew about her friend, Brenda and what a great dressmaker she was. The two of them would often go into the city on Saturdays to buy material to make dresses for the dances, even though that meant them having to walk to work the following week. My mother liked a little excitement, even a little anarchy and when it wasn't coming her way, she liked to create it.

Back in 1960, in Dublin, there was an air of restlessness around the place, a general kind of feeling of something about to happen, or that people were ready for change. I might be only imagining this in retrospect. It might just have been that the winter was over and I had the scent of spring and summer in my nostrils. It could also have been that I was hovering on the edge of being a teenager. In any case, my eyes were starting to move towards the world outside. All the girls were very interested in the new types of clothes that had arrived in Dublin. We knew of people who had travelled to Northern Ireland where they bought different and more casual clothes for girls, like Levi jeans and printed shirts. They had got them from shops called C&As, Marks & Spencer and British Home Stores. None of these English shops were in Dublin then. The clothes they brought back were like nothing we'd seen before – they were for young people, different to what our mothers and fathers wore. Up to that time, there had only been clothes for children and clothes for adults. Here was our opportunity to see if any of those new styles had come to the Dublin shops. My mother wouldn't normally have had any money to buy new clothes then, but she did believe that 'you're only young once'. Her own version of this was 'to hell with poverty, let's kill a chicken'.

As we rarely visited town, I was feeling disorientated and nervous as we started off down towards O'Connell Street. I was awed by the sheer size of the buildings and the different feel of the place, but it was the smells that hit me first. The air had a smoky flavour to it, a mixture of car and bus fumes, burning coal, and a strange smell (later discovered to be from the Guinness factory). The level of activity in the streets too was unfamiliar, not just the sound of the traffic or the carts rattling over cobble stones, but the sound of hundreds of pairs of shoes stomping and walking on the footpaths, people going in different directions, coats swishing, people talking, paper boys yelling out their wares, barrels being dropped down into cellars of pubs, lots of different activities, very different to where we lived.

We crossed O'Connell Bridge, with both of us holding our mother's hands tightly, fearful of falling between the gaps in the bridge's balustrade into the grey, restless river below. Even though spring had arrived, there was a cold wind sweeping up the river taking bites out of us. We half ran, half walked beside our mother, who was moving with unusual determination towards Henry Street. This part of town was even noisier, with street traders and vans and lorries delivering goods. It was here that we got our first glimpse of another, more colourful, world. The shop windows displayed mannequins dressed in trim neat suits in spring colours, fur coats and evening dresses.

Once inside the shop, we were warm. Before us were racks of brightly coloured dresses and coats and 'separates' as they were called. Now, in this delicious time before we had to make up our minds, we wandered around looking at everything. After a while, my mother told us to sit down and the assistant came over to us. We showed her some of the dresses we liked. In the changing room, it felt strange to take off my clothes in a public place. My sister held the curtain closed while I changed and I did the same for her. We tried on the new clothes with speed just in case the shop assistant might open the curtain and ask us if we wanted any help. We didn't want her to see us in our underwear. However, once dressed up in our new finery, we were no longer worried and started to pose as if we were models. Looking at ourselves in the full-length mirror, we stood with our hands on our hips, one knee slightly bent, and a kind of bored look on our faces. Our old clothes lay forlornly on the floor like lifeless little animals. We would have liked to have left them there, but we had to put them on again to go home.

We were each bought a dress and matching cardigan. We moved on from Cassidy's shop to Tyler's to buy shoes. This was on the corner of Abbey Street and O'Connell Street. As we sat silently beside our mother on the shop sofa, we couldn't take our eyes off the light-coloured, frivolous sandals that were displayed with their dainty little straps and buckles. While we imagined and slightly envied the kind of life where the wearing of those sandals was normal and not of any consequence, we were not unpleased with the brown, hard-wearing summer sandals our mother eventually bought us. Our feet felt surprisingly light in them, almost as if we were barefooted. Before going into the shop we hadn't noticed anything in particular about our own winter shoes, but now they looked bashed and worn in comparison to our smart, new ones.

Our next stop was Clery's shop to get tennis racquets. We went downstairs into the basement. It was darker down there, with no windows. It wasn't as glamorous as the other shops because it was mainly full of household objects. We'd never had a tennis racquet before, but the previous year, tennis had been all the rage on our road. We had borrowed racquets, 'had a go' of someone else's, or else sat on the kerb watching the others play. This year, we would have our own. We couldn't believe the extent of our good fortune. We had never been bought so many purchases at the one time before. We went on to Cafolla's café and had an ice cream, all the time giggling, feeling slightly guilty and a bit strange. I kept taking quick glimpses of the new dress in the bag, hoping I'd made the best choice.

We got a different bus home, which stopped outside our school. Without thinking, we got off the bus at the same time as school was finished. Children and teachers were pouring out. As luck would have it, we bumped into our Irish dancing teacher. She spotted my sister and me and walked over to us.

"Where were the two of you this morning?" she asked in a very cross voice. "Why were you both not in today?" she demanded. We hung our heads, both in embarrassment because of all the children around who could hear, and because we didn't know what to say. My heart was pounding. "You ruined the whole performance and we had no one to put in your place for the competition," she said. "What was so important that you had to let the whole class down? All that practicing gone to waste! Well, I hope you have some good excuse, or you need not bother coming to my class again." She left us standing there with our faces burning. Because of the number of people on the footpath, she didn't see our mother who was walking a little ahead of us.

We didn't tell our mother immediately but when we did, she said, "Sure, don't be worrying. You're only young once and you should enjoy yourself." She spoke in a distracted voice and a slight frown had begun to appear on her face. I tried to put what the teacher said out of my mind, but I didn't quite manage it. I felt very tired when we got home, and I didn't feel quite as pleased with myself and my life as I had earlier in the day.

Mariad Whisker

Tangled up in Blue

I never walked the shore at Holywood again, after that.

I wish it had never happened. Or that it had happened somewhere else. Beirut. Vietnam. East LA perhaps. Places I could obliterate like magic with the flick of a remote control. I wish he hadn't told me about it. That sticky July night never goes away.

Nothing is exempt from the unexpected – the consequences of chance, ingredients that come together with no obligation to be anything but random. Chance can shower down disaster with one hand or sprinkle fairy dust with the other. Chance is arbitrary. Unlike intuition.

☐

Glebe House, all gabled Victoriana, stood sentinel over the beach. It held sway over all it surveyed, confident that, bar a cataclysm of biblical proportions, its view would never be compromised. A Gothic window, jutting from its blue slated roof like the shuttered lens of a Hassleblad, documented history as it passed by in great ships, up and down the lough. Behind the rose tinted panes lay its own history, stacked in the attic in dusty boxes that would never reveal their contents.

During stormy days, windblown on its craggy perch, the house seemed to shiver sometimes in its solitude. But in the last lazy days of summer, fading rays from the sun would ricochet off the red brick and conjure up a shadow house that rippled bronze on the water's edge.

Belfast Lough on foggy days melded with the open sea. On brighter days, the sun honed its contours, outlining Carrickfergus as it crept up the northern side, hardened grey. Holywood on the southern bank was softer, fringed with its band of mottled oyster sand.

Carrickfergus held no appeal. A one horse town saddled in orange, with its kerbs painted red, white and blue. I kept my distance. Holywood on the other hand, even with its missing L, conjured up day-dreams of silver screens with platinum blondes, green gables, black beauties, and yellow brick roads. Starry-eyed notions from a more innocent time.

Glebe House exuded a sturdy presence like a character in a movie of its own. Resolute like *Citizen Kane*, it headlined its loughside setting with a verdant cast of elm and silver birch in supporting roles. I loved its pugnacious bearing, its windswept isolation. But more than that I loved it for playing host to my love affair with Jimmy Barbour.

The house belonged to his friend, John. We nick-named him Steed after the guy in *The Avengers*. Steed had inherited the house from a wealthy uncle who died childless and intestate. He kept it much as it was in his uncle's day, though not quite as pristine.

A sophisticated uncle. The house was testament to that. He had a penchant for thirties glamour, jazz and Cubist art which he cultivated along with a collection of musical instruments. Tubas, cellos and trombones masqueraded as sculptures throughout the house. Maquettes of Art Deco buildings, never built, collected dust on plinths along the hallway. The house was crammed with objets d'art, the kind that gets to be displayed and appreciated in a home that boasts of no children. It was an homage to taste and style in its day.

Its grandeur had faded somewhat but the house was a special place. Not just because I spent that last enchanted summer there with Jimmy. Glebe House was a secret from the outside world. It could be approached only from the shore or from down a private lane that led from the main road. In the summertime the lane was canopied by great elms. Primroses embroidered the mossy banks under tangles of hawthorn and bramble. The house lay beyond a delapidated wooden gate and the driveway was perpetually overgrown with rhododendrons. Purple fuchsia commandeered what little garden was left.

After leaving the graffitied breezeblock and muraled pebble-dash of West Belfast, it was magical to enter that hidden copse. To venture from the garden to the house, through the whimsy of its innards, to where the lough light flooded its facade. We would laze around on the granite steps that spilled down the garden to the shore. Steed and Jimmy on guitar and Wild Turkey. Val and me on Blue Nun. Even now, I hear my footsteps crunching seashells in contrast to the slapping rhythm of the water. Even now I feel Jimmy's touch, smell the leather of his vintage trenchcoat. Taste his salty kiss.

☐

Strangely, it was Steed I had my eye on first. I spotted him in college sauntering towards the back tables of the cafeteria where all the Fine Artists hung out. Coolville, we called it. He had a plate of baked beans in one hand and a bottle of Coca Cola in the other. He was wearing Levis. Like James Dean. All the other guys wore bell-bottom loons from Kensington Market. Steed was swoon material, but it wasn't until he performed at the Fresher's Concert that I really fell for him.

He walked on stage in his skinny jeans and a shrunken denim jacket. His curly hair hung halfway down his back under a black Stetson. He wore lizard skin cowboy boots with Cuban heels and had a guitar slung over his shoulder. He was smoking a Marlboro.

The smoke plumed under the brim of the cowboy hat and blurred his face. He had to squint for the few electric moments it took to tune his guitar. But the killer moment was when he sucked a last drag from the cigarette, took it from his lips and stuck it between the end frets of the guitar. And then tore into *Tangled up in Blue*. He did Dylan better than Dylan did himself in my book. I was sent.

He was too. But not for me, unfortunately. He had spotted my friend, Valerie, in the crowd and after the concert made a bee-line for her. They made out all night and I made do with some Graphics geek. Next morning in the cafeteria, Valerie was going on and on about what a great kisser he was when in he ambled with his friend. They got some coffee and as they sidled past our table Steed paused,

"Wanna come to Lucy Jennings' party tonight?"

"Sure. Why not. Can I bring my friend? This is Katie."

"If you like." He shrugged, nodded towards his friend. "This is Jimmy."

Jimmy gave us a cursory glance, hesitated for a second then wandered on down to Coolville. A no-fly zone for freshers like us.

"Meet you 'bout eight in Kelly's Cellars then."

Steed gave Valerie a friendly little dig on the shoulder and a deadly wink. I winced. Then he walked away. Valerie spent the rest of the break wondering which belly jumper to wear with her velvet loons. I gazed over her shoulder checking out Jimmy, wondering what he would be wearing.

I fell in love with him that night. He was in Kelly's Cellars alone when I arrived. There was no sign of Steed or Valerie. It was awkward. I sat down on the bench beside him, leaving lots of space between us. He was making mini sculptures with the silver paper from his cigarette packet. I didn't recognise the brand. A slick black box with gilt writing. I was trying to read the name when he said,

"You want one?"

"What are they?"

"Cigarettes." He flipped the box towards me with a snap of his middle finger.

His tone was perfunctory.

"I meant, what kind?"

"The coffin kind. What other kind is there?"

I wanted to run.

"Coughing nails. At least they're pretty." He flicked the box open.

"Have one. Choose your favourite colour."

The cigarettes were so pretty I was taken aback. I leaned in towards him to get a closer look. Each one was a different colour, orange, turquoise, lilac, jade, all with gold filters. Like a box of painter's pastels.

"Sobranie Cocktail. Pretty, but lethal. Go on, have one."

I didn't smoke but I took one anyway. The jade one. He leaned over and lit it for me with a flip-top brass lighter. The kind they used in *M*A*S*H*. I inhaled too deeply and started choking. It was like sand-paper in my throat. I coughed and spluttered so violently that I had to stumble out in to the street for air. He followed a few minutes later carrying my white fringed-leather shoulder bag and a glass of water. I sensed he was smirking.

"You want some water?"

I shook my head. My face was roaring red. My eyes were streaming. I took my bag from him and rummaged for a handkerchief.

"C'mon, you need some air. You can't go back in there. Let's walk."

"What about Valerie and Steed?" I mumbled into my hanky. I wanted to go home.

"What about them?"

"But what about Lucy Jennings' party?" I stammered.

"What about it?" He cocked his head a little to the side.

"Who's Lucy Jennings anyway?"

He left the water on the windowsill and started walking. I followed. By the time we reached his flat behind Queen's University, I was holding his hand.

☐

Before long, I left home and moved in with Jimmy. We spent weekdays at college in Belfast and ecstatic weekends at Glebe House. Valerie moved in with Steed and took to playing lady of the manor. We called her Mrs Peel. They rescued a black Alsatian from the pound and we named him Avenger. Jimmy and I would walk him along the shore at Holywood. We would picnic at Helen's Bay. He would read me Baudelaire and Rimbaud in a terrible French accent. I would laugh and pretend to understand.

The year passed too quickly.

I transferred to London. He said he would follow. He didn't. He followed someone else instead. I had bought tickets for a Bowie concert without realising that the date coincided with my brother's wedding in California. I gave the tickets to Jimmy thinking Steed would go with him. Or Valerie, an even bigger fan.

I phoned from San Francisco, eager to hear about the concert. Steed answered, mumbled some lame excuse for not going. Jimmy wasn't there, which led to severe interrogation. Steed buckled easily, spilled the beans. Some ditzy red-head went to the concert with Jimmy instead. One lie led to lots of them. We broke up when I got back from California. Steed felt responsible.

I cried bucketfuls. I got Valerie to spill every bean about the new girl. I read Baudelaire alone in bed at night and smoked Sobranies. I played sappy songs like *Without You* non-stop on my Dansette. Then we all lost touch.

Jimmy faded into the background of my new life in London. I was relieved to have escaped Belfast and its escalating terror. I was happy in the smoky anonymity of the big city, despite being drip-fed daily by the tabloids with news of the bombs and carnage at home. I was grateful not to have become fodder for the beast that had possessed poor old Belfast.

Eventually, I was relieved to be free of Jimmy too. As London opened up to me, the crack that he made closed over. I didn't see him anymore – in my dreams, or out.

☐

Until one day Steed called me. Out of the blue.

☐

The road to Holywood had been my Sunset Boulevard. It had swept me out and away from the darkening heart of Belfast into a fable of my own. It looped around the past – the shrinking shipyard with its giant offspring, Samson and his smaller brother, Goliath, striking steely yellow poses by the lough. More for tourists, than for ocean-going liners. Still smarting from the tattered legacy of the Titanic. And more recent stuff.

It took me out past those wastelands of long dead industry, into wetlands that favoured lapwings, oyster catchers and corncrakes. Curlews wheeled over the marsh, as the road-beat morphed from the thwack of concrete to a tar-macadammed hum. The black ribbon laced through scalloped hedges that hid fancy mansions. Gone with the wind, I would sometimes be so engrossed as Scarlett that I would miss the turn-off down to Glebe House.

This time I hadn't.

I was driving to Holywood at Steed's request. I was home to celebrate my twenty first birthday with my family. Steed called me, asked me to come visit. He put Valerie on the line to persuade me. I knew that Jimmy had moved into Glebe House permanently. I had my own grapevine. Steed hinted that something bad happened to Jimmy. I was sorry to hear that. But really – I didn't want to know.

I had distanced myself from the aches and pains of Belfast. I had no desire to re-open wounds of any kind. Steed assured me there would be no risk of that. I believed him. The following day I borrowed Millie, my sister's battered Morris Minor, and drove to Holywood. The drive was as lovely as ever. Shards of sunlight strobed through the leafy tunnel down to Glebe House. I could smell the sea as I nosed Millie through the tangled fuchsia. I felt a lurch. In my chest. I blamed it on the lumpy clutch. I took my foot off the brake and felt the lurch again. The blame could have gone either way.

The back door was open as usual. My runners squeaked on the tiles but Steed didn't hear me come in. I found him alone, on the living room floor, working on a model aeroplane. His face was a mask of concentration. His hair was short. The room looked shabbier than I remembered. Saucers of cat food lay crusting in the corners. There was no sign of Avenger. Steed looked up startled, then stepped carefully over his aeroplane and bounded over towards me. He hugged me, told me I didn't look a day over twenty one. I hugged him back. I thought he wasn't looking too bad himself.

"My new hobby," he said. "Building them instead of painting them."

We made some small talk. Nothing important. Then he nodded towards the window overlooking the lough. He shrugged his shoulders, made a helpless gesture with his hands. I looked out. I saw Jimmy in the distance, blurred by the dried salt crystals that caked the window. Recognised his matchstick figure, greyed further by a low mist rolling in from the sea. Steed took my hand and walked me to the front porch.

A cloud crept across the sun. The garden looked sad and gloomy. A smattering of sand blown up by a recent storm had pooled in mini dunes on the steps. I could see the imprints of Jimmy's Converse sneakers all the way down to the water.

"He's messed up, you know." Steed toed his cowboy boot into the corner of the top step, wrecking a sand dune.

"So, what's new?"

"I'm not joking, Katie. He's in bits."

"She must have been something then."

"It's not about a girl. Is that what you think?"

"I presumed, I guess. What else was I to think?"

"It's pretty bad."

"Oh come on, Steed. It can't be that bad, for Chrissake."

"It's as bad as it gets in this fucking hell-hole."

"Then I'm not sure I want to hear about it."

"Well, Val and I thought seeing you might help him."

I laughed.

"Yeah right. And when you're writing home about it, tell me why I would want to help Jimmy bloody Barbour?"

"He's a victim too, Katie."

"Well that's hardly my fault, is it?"

"Don't be so hard on him. Please? I swear he doesn't need that."

"Jesus, Steed. That's what Belfast's all about, isn't it? Victims. That's why I left. I escaped."

"Count your lucky stars then. 'Cause not everybody did. Especially not Jimmy."

I shivered.

He wrapped his arms around my shoulders and kissed the top of my head, with a tenderness that made me shiver more. Perhaps it was just the chilly breeze. I held on to his hand as I walked down the steps. I was loathe to let go. By the time I reached the bottom step our fingertips trailed apart.

The wind flung sand against my bare legs. I wished I'd worn my jeans. It was August but the day had squandered all its warmth. Seagulls screamed like banshees. A ferryboat steamed up the lough towards the open sea. The Larne-Stranraer. Full of Belfast people like me I presumed. Escaping.

The sea shells crunched beneath my sneakers, softer than I remembered. Jimmy sensed me before he heard me. He was making marks in the dowdy sand with a piece of driftwood. When he turned around and saw me, he just stood there. He gazed at me like I wasn't there at all. As I got closer, I saw that he was crying. He did nothing to stop the tears. Didn't wipe them away. Just let them run down his cheeks without shame. I felt awkward. I remembered that first night in Kelly's Cellars. My instinct to run.

I put my arms around him when his tears turned into guttural, wracking sobs. He cried enough tears for Holywood. For all of Belfast. For the whole of Northern Ireland. But mostly he cried for the kid who got shot that clammy July evening. The boy who shuddered against his chest. The boy whose head he tried to hold together with his hands. And comfort with his arms until the army came. His embrace was futile.

It took me years to realize that my embrace was futile too.

Jennifer Mary Brown

These Hours in the Cellar

I'm putting on your winter
warmers, piece by piece:

glasses with horned-rim fade,
fingerless gloves with mitten

flaps, a holey Brooks Brothers
scarf, and a grey Irish cap.

They gang up and I'm gone.
You lose layers of wool but

gain empty bottles of Budweiser.
Airy laughter wins over mild

chatting, so I say, in your things,
"I am you now. You must be me."

You only say, "You're not me.
I have man parts and a beard.

If I'm you I need girl arms and
your legs for days." Together we

claim a mass of chicken bones
and orange hot sauce-covered

lips, but also lose weight in
our wallets, vigour in our knees.

Later, as we exit up the stairs,
I'm left in your cap but you say,

"You better lose that too, or I'll
gain an appeal for newsboys."

I shake my hair out from under it,
curls dropping, and hand it over.

Now Please Remove your Clothing

Inanimate objects are fearless,
so let's swap clothes for a few
weeks until we meet again.

I want your most worn, your
most unwashed items. The ones
you grab off the floor some morning.

Like that orange plaid cowboy
shirt you wore every day the last
week we were in New Jersey.

You won't miss it, and you get
that blue shirt with the hem
of ribbon around the collar.

In my clothes, feel free to wait
and wander around, to sleep all
morning and drink coffee in

my red-striped knee socks, dance
your way across my kitchen,
longing like the lover I am, wear

my grey and pink hot-shorts.
You can take my tailored jeans
to see some Etruscan architecture.

I'll wear your Satan On The Moon
t-shirt on a walk in Phoenix Park,
drink a Guinness in your coat.
In your baggy jeans I'll stroll,

shaking hands with neighbours,
enjoying negative shapes like you.

In the street we'll catch ourselves on
each other, I'll see my green suede
flats with their rain-damaged folds.

You can spot me from afar
by your black wool sweater.
Your shoes will return me to you.

The Comedy of Heart Disease
for Charles Bukowski

You have low blood pressure, so I wait
and worry sometimes until dawn listening
to you breathe next to me with your arms
in folds under my legs, hands over knees.

It's silly, other times, when we stand
nose to nose near the back bar stools
and you're a Silverback gorilla beating
your chest with the side of your fist.

So I match your furrowed brow until you
say Baby, punch me please? and I wind
up like I'm Goose Gossard but deliver a neat,
centred finger-poke to the breast bone

and you scowl, you are serious, and I let
you have it: a punch from your girl with two
beers in her. You jump, mouth, eyes wide
open and say Darlin', you hit me *so* hard.

The Wind Picks Up On the Way to the Bar

Let the wind wrap around your legs, but
first, over the big wheel with its broken spoke,
then through to bare knees and up
your paisley dress, floating then, hovering,

intrepid air. Don't question, just absorb it,
just live it, just let it glide you through.
Rocks, should they trap under you, will spit
out behind, down the middle of the gritty

gravel street. The one that has special highs
and lows to slow speed that you can
anticipate through the darkness. You are
a Chiaroscuro painting, an illustrious body

swimming with no mind, no back log,
no creative eternal memory. You're just you
listening to the song whipping into your ears
from the wind passing by leaving no trace.

My Guide to Relational Success

Just wet your lips and curl your tongue in,
lengthwise. Don't touch the sides together.
Only let your lips tighten when you have a sound.

Flatten the middle of your tongue,
curl the back up and the front sort of down,
but don't touch the roof of your mouth.

Whirl air through the gap in your two front teeth,
but slow enough that you can control
the whistling noise that comes out.

Now move your tongue back and forth
while keep previous muscles contracted
to control pitch and volume.

Keep this delicate balance of muscles
and breath, while continually listening
to your sound; live inside its pitch.

Drive home on a back road, listen
to music with harmonica solos and laugh
with your sweetheart between tracks.

Forming a New Waddle

I wish I had winked at him on the sidewalk
that evening when he said he had
a penguin-shaped hole in his chest
whenever I wasn't around.

Earlier, us giggling almost lovers outside
a bullet-proof tiny habitat, a glass jar
bombed by those quick diving, fluffed feathers
of the Antarctic that I imitated all afternoon.

In a small moat, still adorable in desperation,
arching performing sea lions abound!
The unkempt yard of a single polar bear;
atheists on the Sabbath as we were.

He scratched his beard and we strolled,
I hiked up my plaid skirt with brown ruffles,
him in a grey cardigan and Irish cap,
itchy brown fake wool socks to my knees.

Down Park Avenue, a Saturday afternoon
in October, at the same age
we looked like a May-December.

(At the zoo, months before the
real beginning, when my
flushed bursting heart fit in that
aquatic hole inside of his.)

Become a Creature

What to have instead of a home
is a giant luminous lagoon,
like that one in that dream I had
where a shark-shaped two-headed

sea monster swallowed my dad while
he smiled and waved, wearing
a yellow bandana around his neck.
Besides the death of dad, the lagoon

was a pale aqua misty orb, floating
in a sac like a water bed, and my
family were all headed in and out
and all around it, talking loud.

Just tend to the algae bloom and let
the fish inside roam freely, skim out
the accidental trash left by you, drunk
one night floating on an inner tube.

On Art

But you're prettier
than Jesus!
Which Jesus?
Italian Jesus?

No, more like
German Jesus.

No one can
aspire to be
prettier than Italian
Jesus, Baby.

Claire Coughlan

Maria Maria

Every day, throughout the month of May, one of the little girls from the house next door lit a candle in front of Her. The chipped and pockmarked plaster had been sanded and smoothed by Tom, the girls' father; the blue and white paint, which had peeled and flaked like sheaves of dead skin, had received a fresh double coat. Tom, an antiques restorer by trade, often cast his eye over the various bric-a-brac that came into the shop and sometimes he set to work on it but he never charged, as it was – he was always fond of saying – for charity.

She was as good as new, thought Susan, glancing into the front window display as she slid her key into the lock and started the first part of her early morning routine in the shop. She turned the sign to 'We're in business!' switched on all the lights and got a cloth to give all stock a good dusting. Mountains of clothes, books, CDs, vases and jewellery littered the floor and every available surface. Whenever something came in that looked as though it might be of some value, Susan automatically asked Tom for advice. He'd said that the statue was worthless, but had fixed it up anyway at her request – Susan wasn't religious but she'd thought it might be bad luck to throw Her out.

Making her way to the window, she lightly dusted the top of Her head, and left Her in the early morning sunlight, dust motes swirling around Her like fairy dust.

□

...Because she knew she had to; if she didn't leave within the next twenty minutes, anything could happen. Mer dumped a pile of clothes into the suitcase she had found in Bella's room and threw her vanity case in on top of it. Tearing down the narrow stairs, she entered the living room, with its rose patterned wallpaper, oleograph above the black iron mantelpiece and the statue of the Virgin Mary in the near corner, beside the door. Ignoring Bella's doubtlessly unintended irony of having such a statue in a house like this, she grabbed it around the upper part. It was heavier than it looked, but the serenely bowed head fitted imperfectly into her hand nonetheless. She wrapped it in some clothes and placed it in the centre of the suitcase. Blessing herself, she folded her shawl – one of Bella's that she'd taken – around her shoulders, picked up the bag and opened the door for the last time. Looking back up the stairs, she closed it as gently as a mother would have so as not to wake a sleeping child. Outside the night was blacker than Bella's heart. It had just stopped raining and the jumble of cobblestones was slick and greasy. Mer put her head down and walked, praying she wouldn't meet anyone she knew. But apart from the odd sound of revelry coming from any of the nearby kips of Dublin's Nighttown, the darkness kept its secrets. Rounding the corner onto Railway Street, she heard the smash of glass and the familiar screech as a fight broke out, between two girls, by the sounds of it, and probably over business. Thanking Mary and the Sacred Heart that she was almost away from all that now, Mer fled down to Store Street and kept walking from there to the quays. Slowly, slowly. Clinging to the shadows like a demented ghost, she found a vacant and obscure doorway to settle down in before the ship left for New York next morning.

□

...And how dare he speak to her like that anyway, especially after everything she'd given this afternoon. He could stuff his stupid part. She was going to be as late as she pleased. In fact, she was now going for a massage. Norma adjusted her dark glasses and headscarf and gingerly approached the door to her trailer. She paused beside the statue as she passed. She smiled, touching the chipped, blue plaster of the solid, gathered skirts at the bottom. She wasn't even Catholic but liked having it around – it made her feel lucky. Although there hadn't been too much of that around lately, she thought, biting her lip, then lifting her glasses and checking in the mirror behind the statue to make sure there was no lipstick on her front teeth. A cleaner on the studio lot had given it to her, said she was her biggest fan. An Irish woman, had one of those faces that looked as though it had seen a ton. Norma adjusted her cleavage and patted the statue on the head. Opening the door, she paused. "How do you like Sugar now?" she thought, directed at no one in particular amongst the anthill of activity across the studio.

"Marilyn, five minutes and you're up," a voice trickled through her consciousness, like lemon juice being strained through a muslin cloth.

"You'll have to catch me first," she muttered, not quite sure if she'd said it aloud or not.

☐

...Five minutes, that's all he said he'd be. What was taking him so long? Brenda May half heartedly rubbed a smeared glass against her apron and placed it, open end down, on the dusty shelf. She traced the outline of her rectangular jaw with her forefinger and sneezed. The end of summer was in the air and the pollen count was high. Blondie was on the juke box and Debbie Harry's lazily trilled soprano dared her to take the evening off. But she'd better not. Dad had said he wouldn't be too long at the wholesalers.

She walked to the end of the bar and tapped some buttons on the cash register. It opened with a tr-ring! Brenda May extracted ten dollars from the plastic compartment and stuffed it down her bra. She peeked over her shoulder to make sure no one had seen her. Billy 'One Eye' Madison, hunched over his fifth whiskey of the afternoon, winked at her. Brenda May cringed. He was always saying things like: "When are you going to let me buy you a beer, now that you're officially legal?"

Flustered, she swung back around towards the cash register and nudged the statue with the side of her elbow. It shuddered and fell to the dirty lino floor. Brenda May gasped. That statue was her Dad's lucky Mary; if she'd broken it, she might as well leave home right now. A customer who worked on one of the big studio lots had brought it in one night, it had been left in a trailer. Frank, Brenda May's father, had taken a liking to it and gave the guy five dollars for it. Legend had it that it had belonged to Marilyn Monroe and Frank liked to say that if he had to have one broad watching him all the time, better make it Marilyn. That didn't make sense, but Brenda May thought she knew what he meant.

The statue rolled like a gentle wave and settled on its side, the unblinking face gazing calmly towards the cash register, away from the bar. Brenda May gently picked Her up, as though she were nursing a bird with a broken wing, and placed Her back in Her place beside the cash register.

One Eye let out a guffaw. "I won't tell Frank, if you won't! I guess we can both keep a secret!" he leered.

Brenda May twitched one corner of her mouth in what she hoped was a sardonic smile. She turned away and examined Her injuries. Three big chips gone from the front of Her robes and one small one from Her head. But She was still in one piece.

One Eye tapped the side of his glass and winked. Brenda May was just about to tell him he'd had enough, but then, she heard her father's voice say:

"Reckon it's about time to be heading for the hills, don't you Billy?"

"Screw you, Frank," was the cheerful response.

Frank winked at his daughter and walked to the cash register. He glanced at the statue and at Brenda May and wordlessly began counting the day's takings before the evening trade started. Brenda May sighed and scratched her chin. Debbie Harry's voice trembled and the evening stretched ahead. Brenda May remembered the ten dollars in her bra and suddenly the night was a parasol of possibility, just waiting to unfurl.

☐

...A right little madam and the mother didn't seem to do anything about it. Susan went to the window and gently lifted the statue up, as though she were picking up a fretting toddler, carrying Her to the desk on which the cash register rested.

"So, as you can see, it's been restored and is now in mint condition," Susan began her sales pitch.

"How old is it?" interrupted the woman. The child picked up a delicate looking vase and began knocking it against the plywood of the desk. Susan winced.

"Hard to say, but I've had it professionally appraised and we've estimated at around the century mark."

The woman, who had huge bluey-purple eyes, blinked and nodded. Her daughter, who, Susan noticed, had similar eyes, had put down the vase and now, much to Susan's relief, turned her attention to a miniature Russian doll.

"Okay, we'll take it," she declared.

"Don't you want to know how much it is?" Susan wondered.

"Sure. You can tell me while you're wrapping it up."

"It's five hundred euro," Susan improvised.

"Okay. Do you take credit cards?"

"We certainly do."

"I wanna different doll," the little girl suddenly piped up.

Susan frowned.

"This isn't a doll," she said quietly, taking the credit card from the mother with those extraordinary eyes, which were so beautiful they looked like pools of amethyst.

"What is it then?" asked the child, with the same unnerving stare as her mother.

Susan hesitated before swiping the card and, slotting it into the machine, she entered the amount. Was she doing them a terrible wrong, charging this much? Nonsense, she quickly chided herself. The woman hadn't even wanted to know how much it was and the ludicrous amount hadn't even registered with her.

"Now, just enter your PIN there, please," she said, swivelling the machine around to face the woman.

The child obviously wasn't used to being ignored. "What is it if it isn't a doll?"

"Shush now," said her mother. "She's a special kind of doll. I'll tell you on the way home. Your Granny used to have one exactly like it."

Susan smiled and ripped the merchant receipt from the machine, waiting for the customer one to print off.

After a few seconds, it came out and she handed it to Violet Eyes. They both stood there, Susan smiling into space, until she jumped and remembered that she hadn't wrapped the statue.

"I'm sorry, I'll get that wrapped up for you now," she muttered.

"It's alright, we don't need it wrapped. Thanks anyway."

The woman smoothed the arms of her beige mac and tapped the child on the shoulder, who picked up the statue with both hands. They carried it in a procession-like formation out the door, the mother walking solemnly in front, the daughter slowly following, carefully clutching the statue around the middle. She stood so upright, and her hands were aligned so neatly that it looked almost ceremonial.

Susan leaned on the counter and took out a nail file from the container that held her pens. She was sorry to see Her go. But at least she'd got a very good price for what was probably worthless junk. And then, thinking of the five hundred euro she'd just made on Her, she raised the corners of her lips in a whisper of a smile. She'd brought her luck, alright. She couldn't argue with that.

Jennifer McGrath

Boterique

The Pierre family lived in a large *maison de campagne*, on a plateau, on the outskirts of Paris. You could see white capped mountains from every one of its twelve windows. The household consisted of Mrs Mariella Pierre, Grandmére Bette, Uncle Vic and baby Petunia. Alongside these were the stout Catdog, Alberta the maid and the cook Francesco, not forgetting Emile Pierre himself. People in the neighbourhood believed that there was also a madwoman in their attic, but the Pierres had yet to confirm or deny their suspicions.

Mr Pierre worked in Paris as a proof-reader in a publications house. It was a very boring job so he often came home grumpy and tired. People didn't seem to bother with good spelling anymore, they couldn't make sense of apostrophes or commas so they just sent him in any old stuff and let him deal with it. Mr Pierre had been working with the company for five years and had come to hate it.

In the past, the morning routine had begun with Mariella dragging him out of bed, trying to remove his hands from around her waist, buttering him up with the promise of croissants, hot chocolate, sausages and cheese, until after another ten minutes of cuddling, he finally dressed and made his way downstairs. As the realisation hit him that he would have to spend another day in work, he would sit mute and scowling as Mariella chatted away to her mother about the weather and the cost of stockings. After listlessly attempting to eat the breakfast cooked by Francesco, Emile got a lift into the city with his brother, Marco.

After the baby's arrival, however, Mr Pierre raced downstairs and darted red-faced from the door without even waving goodbye. He didn't want to think about what had happened to his brother and he didn't want to have to talk to Mariella. He knew she would soon be sitting upstairs in the front window, fingers clinging to her black handkerchief, eyes blank and fixed, as she had done every day since it happened. All he wanted to do was hide.

□

Marco Pierre had been a member of the household ever since the birth of his niece, Petunia. The day of her birth was one he would not forget. He was just about to leave the bakery he owned when he received the great news. His sister-in-law, Mariella, had given birth to a beautiful baby girl. On entering the maternity ward, he was confronted with the image of his older brother, Emile, asleep on the floor underneath a chair. Emile had a tendency to do this in times of stress. Not surprisingly, Marco felt embarrassed to see his thirty five year old brother lying curled up in the middle of a hospital corridor. He nudged him awake and Emile yawned and stretched. "Let's go in and see your daughter shall we?" Marco asked, grabbing his brother by the shoulder. Emile nodded sheepishly.

Mariella looked exhausted, which wasn't surprising as the baby was huge. It lay on its mother's chest playing with her hair, trying to chew on its own fingers. It wasn't the prettiest baby, as its cheeks protruded and its eyes were tiny and very far apart. Marco could see that it wasn't going to be a smart child, but he couldn't say that. Emile was already a nervous wreck and implying that the child had some kind of mental disability would not go down well.

"She's beautiful," Marco said, "Congratulations."

He moved in to touch the baby and it turned to face him and smiled. He stuck out a finger for the baby to grab and it did so, shoving the finger in its gummy mouth and sucking on it vigorously. Uncle Vic and Grandmére Bette laughed and so did Mariella.

"She has the reflexes of a cat," Marco remarked, trying not to blush from the pain. He could feel the tip of his finger going numb. Emile smiled.

After a couple of weeks, mother and baby Petunia came home. They would have been home sooner but Mariella, who had always been rather slender and pale, had developed anaemia and had to be well rested and 'fattened up' to ensure her strength returned. Emile was not pleased about this development as his wife was already a good foot and a half taller than he was and with the help of the hospital staff, she was now also considerably larger than him in terms of girth. It made him look ridiculous. But of course, he couldn't let on. Whenever she asked him how she looked, he'd give the same reply he always had: "Lumineuse." Mariella didn't mind the repetition of his answer, she liked consistency and she loved her new, more voluptuous, figure.

☐

Over the coming months, Marco spent less and less time in work. Soon after the arrival of his daughter, Emile had confided in him that all was not well at home. He no longer felt any attraction to his wife and he wasn't very fond of his daughter either. To put it mildly. Petunia was unbearably clingy and extremely wilful. She grew quicker than any other child they had ever seen. In the first three weeks she had already gone through four Babygros and had escaped from her cot six times. Emile would wake up with the now one year old Petunia lying between himself and his wife. He felt horrible for feeling nothing but disgust as he gazed at the bloated, ugly face of his daughter as she drooled and muttered in her sleep. Feelings of inadequacy and frustration filled his mind with strange dreams of flying pigs whose entrails fell from the sky, littering the streets of Paris, or of running up a never-ending staircase being chased by Petunia who was foaming at the mouth.

Marco tried not to laugh at his brother, who had always been given to theatrics. He reassured him that things would get better and that it was normal to have bad dreams when big changes were going on. He offered to ease the situation by coming to baby-sit when he could escape from the bakery and suggested they employ someone to look after Petunia in the mornings and afternoons. Mariella consented to the hiring of a maid. Her name was Alberta; a dark haired sixty-year-old German woman who tended not to speak much. She gave the impression of being a strict disciplinarian and got on well with the family, particularly Uncle Vic.

With these changes in place, the house began to return to pre-Petunia normality. Mariella had time to cook and clean and began to paint still-lifes instead of just reading romance novels all day. Grandmére Bette and Uncle Vic were happier as they weren't disturbed by Petunia's violent temper tantrums. Catdog was happy as he could sleep in the larder and gorge on cheese without having to constantly watch out for Petunia.

And Marco enjoyed his evenings with Mariella and the baby. He helped them perform puppet shows as well as reading fairytales to Petunia who had christened him 'Marro'. So while Emile was spending late nights poring over pages of bad punctuation and infantile grammar or sitting daydreaming in bars, his brother was tucking Petunia into bed and singing her a lullaby before forcibly removing his fingers from her mouth. When Mariella noticed the bite marks and the missing fingernails, Marco told her he had had an accident at work. Mariella was happy to have the company of a charming younger man even if it was her husband's brother.

Like all good things however, their idyllic peace had to come to an end. Some weeks later, Emile arrived home with the sense that something was wrong. On walking into the hall he saw blood dripping down the stairs. Following the trail out through the kitchen he found the family sitting at the patio table drinking tea. They never drank tea apart from after funerals. Emile stared at Mariella's ashen face. Her mouth opened to speak but no words came out.

"Ze Catdog," Grandmére Bette snarled: "ze animal has finally done eet, I always knew ze cat vas too big, he is like giant warthog, ze fangs on him, he eez a beast!"

She pointed to the kennel her hand trembling. Emile tiptoed over to Catdog's kennel and looked inside. Catdog was chained up and looked angry and put out. His usually pristine white whiskers were pink.

"Why is he chained up?" Emile shouted. He loved Catdog as a loyal childhood friend and hated seeing him bound like a common house pet. Grandmére Bette started muttering in angry German. "What's going on?" Emile asked again, turning away from Bette to Uncle Vic, "Where's Marco?" Mariella broke down into tears.

Uncle Vic said that by the time he got upstairs there was nothing he could do. Emile loved Vic like his own father and the tears rimming his uncle's eyelashes scared him. He began to climb the stairs, following the blood trail on the carpet. It diverged on the landing. He entered Petunia's bedroom and gazed at his little angel. She was immaculate and snoring, tucked up in her bed. Emile sighed with relief and began to head back out of the room, but when he heard Petunia snort and turn in her sleep, he moved back towards her. He peered at the inside of the blanket; it was stained with blood. Gently he lifted it up and to his horror found Marco's head clasped between his daughters pudgy arms.

Where was the rest of him? he wondered, replacing the blanket. Following the other trail into Mariella's room, he found his brother's legs and torso. The left arm was missing from the elbow down. Emile ran downstairs and returned to the kennel. He unchained Catdog who strutted off, glaring at Grandmére Bette (who he felt always had a grudge against him) and made for the larder, his bum high in the air. The family sat motionless.

Emile climbed into the kennel, hugged his knees to his chest and clamped his eyes shut. There he lay for three hours until Catdog came over to lick his face, thus waking him. Emile crawled out, glad that the patio was now empty. Catdog slunk past him, swishing his long black tail and on retrieving an object from the back of his kennel, settled into a comfortable position. Emile could hear him munching and crunching something and turned back to see a fingerless hand covered in drool. The exposed bone jutting out from the darkness seemed to glow in the moonlight.

☐

After Marco's 'disappearance' the silence in the already reticent house became unbearable. Francesco quit, as no one seemed to want to eat anymore except Petunia; well, that was the official reason. The actual reason was that he was tired of the constant questioning he was subjected to by everyone in the neighbourhood and of the sleep-deprived Emile's worsening mood. Petunia, bereft of her favourite uncle, was acting up again and consequently no one was happy. On top of this, Grandmére Bette moved back to Germany, as she was convinced she was next on Catdog's list.

Emile could no longer ignore the burgeoning fears his daughter created in him but he couldn't say anything to Mariella about it. His wife was stuck like a record, asking him how work was, how his day was and what he had for lunch, would he be home late, etc etc. Emile tried as best he could to answer her questions but they were slowly driving him mad. He knew she had changed and that she wasn't really listening; her eyes barely registered his presence. He was sickened to discover that she could paint only one recurring image. That of a smiling Marco, with bite marks on his left hand, which was missing three fingernails. When she fell asleep, Emile would hide the finished paintings under a box in the larder.

☐

At the age of four, Petunia started school and the house filled with hope. Maybe she would make friends, get some discipline and the attention she craved. And school actually *was* great for her. She enjoyed sports and games, but she wasn't really into maths or reading. She liked other kids and became less clingy. Emile buried himself in his work as usual and only remembered that he had a daughter when the letter telling them about the parent-teacher meeting arrived. This news lifted Mariella's spirits and she persuaded Emile to accompany her.

Petunia's teacher was a young woman called Mademoiselle Vermont. She had many questions about the child; was it happy at home? Who was Marro? Was there an athlete in the family? Emile left Mariella to do the talking.

"Petunia is happy and healthy, she is happy at home," she said, a saccharine smile spreading across her face.

"And who is Marro?" the teacher asked.

"I have no idea".

"Oh." The teacher blushed and looked down at her clipboard. "I'm afraid we've had a few problems with Petunia," she almost whispered.

"Oh?"

"Yes, we've noticed that she is slightly aggressive with the other children, but we don't know if that's just to do with her size or age."

Mariella's eyes burned.

"What do you mean her size?"

"Just that she's a little larger than most of the children. What age is she?"

"I don't know what you mean," Mariella barked, "She's four and a half."

"I didn't mean to offend you." The teacher began to sweat. "Has she seen a doctor recently?"

"There's no reason for her to see a doctor. She's perfectly healthy."

With that, Mariella stood up, knocking over her chair and grabbed her bag roughly.

"Excuse me, we have to be going, my husband is due back at work."

When they arrived home Mariella ran inside calling to Petunia, but there was no answer. She ran around searching every room but she couldn't find the child anywhere. Emile sat on the sofa and rubbed his bloodshot eyes. Uncle Vic came in from the kitchen.

"What's that racket?" he asked, "Why is she screaming like that?"

"Oh, she can't find the baby, have you seen her?"

"Not since I put her to bed for her nap about two hours ago," Vic replied, "I'll go look for her." Emile nodded, he didn't really care where Petunia was, he just wanted to sleep, to postpone another working day. He decided to go talk to Catdog before he went to bed. Peering out the kitchen window, he saw that the kennel was empty. He knew where the fat cat would be.

"I found her," Uncle Vic shouted.

"Petunia? Petunia! Where's my baby?" Mariella called from the top of the stairs. Vic opened the larder door and Emile gasped. There, lying in a pool of blood, was Petunia, clutching what looked like a long black rope. She had torn all the faces out of the paintings with her bloodied nails. Vic hoisted Petunia up and she awoke, dropping the rope. Vic handed her to Mariella as Emile slammed the door shut behind him.

"Oh my baby, what a mess!" she exclaimed, taking Petunia upstairs to bathe her, "who was playing in the jam, eh? Or were you painting?"

Emile bent down to pick up the rope-like object and realised that it was Catdog's tail. It was covered in little bite marks and most of the fur was gone. He grabbed a bin bag, cleaned up the remains and mopped up the blood. In a matter of minutes, he had dug a hole in the garden and thrown in the heavy bag. Changing his clothes, he told Mariella he was going back to work. She nodded but didn't reply. She was mesmerised, watching the black hairs that were collecting around the plughole.

□

When Emile returned from work, the house was quiet again. He walked into his bedroom and saw Petunia on his side of the bed and Mariella on the other. Both of them were drooling and snoring loudly. He went in to sleep in what was Grandmére Bette's room. It felt cold and damp. He didn't fall asleep until after four and was plagued by dreams in which his daughter played with Marco's headless corpse as if it was a rag doll, throwing it against the walls and laughing as the eyeballs rolled around the floor. He woke before six.

Creeping into his room and grabbing his suitcase, he filled it with clothes and tiptoed downstairs. Alberta arrived soon after and set about cleaning the house. Emile always liked her; she didn't really talk. Like him she was not a morning person. She kept to herself, stayed with them despite the rumours, and cleaned up any spills, no questions asked. She seemed to love Petunia and was the only one who could control her despite the fact the girl was now about double the size of her. Emile nodded a good morning to Alberta and she nodded back. He sat and drank his coffee, even though it had long ago ceased to have any effect on his fatigue. Bidding Alberta a goodbye, he headed outside. After laying a flower down on Catdog's grave, Emile said a prayer.

The neighbours were starting to come out of their houses and heading off to work, so he moved quickly to the car. He had always hated Marco's station wagon, there was no need for such a big car. He hated the shape of it, but it was good to have all the same. As he climbed in, he could hear someone wailing. It was Petunia yelling for him, for her Papa. He turned around to see her, clad in a buttermilk petticoat, positioned dangerously on the windowsill. Alberta's face was lined from stress and her forehead was beaded with sweat from the exertion of trying to hold Petunia back from the open window. Her scrawny arms were barely getting around the huge girl's chest. Emile could see Uncle Vic's head peering out a side window, the remnants of shaving foam still visible around the edges of his black moustache.

Petunia moved closer to the open window, her feet on the ledge. Alberta broke her unspoken bond of silence and called out to Emile for help. Her voice was low and hoarse; it reminded him of his grandmother's. Emile waved to Petunia who became even more frantic. And then it happened. She fell, her head smashing against the wide, concrete doorsteps, with a thud.

Emile didn't know if it had actually happened or whether it was just one of his dreams. But he turned back and there was Petunia, lying spread eagled on the steps. Alberta had disappeared from view and a moment later, Mariella appeared in her favourite window and sat looking out. Clutching her black handkerchief, she gazed blankly at the road, her eyes glazed over. Dead. Emile could hear Alberta sobbing and Uncle Vic asking what the racket was.

He drove on.

Notes on the Writers

Colin Barrett was born in Canada and grew up in Mayo. He has a BA in English from UCD. His short story, 'Let's Go Kill Ourselves', will appear in a forthcoming issue of *The Stinging Fly*.

Jennifer Mary Brown is too sweet for Rock and Roll, but luckily she's an artist with clashing instincts. She received her BA in English and Studio Art from the University of Vermont. There, she was the Art Student of the Year in 2005. *A Return to Mother's Love*, a collaborative book featuring her photographs, was published in 2007. She has claimed residence in both New Jersey and Vermont, but now finds herself bounding up and down the east coast and floating around central Europe.

Anne Coughlan began writing many years ago and first attended a Creative Writing class at the Listowel Writer's Week in 1984. The pressures of family and her work as a researcher put her writing on the back boiler until 2001, when she attended Creative Writing courses with the late poet Dorothy Molloy. Since then, Anne has been writing and attending writing workshops on poetry and fiction. She is currently a part-time lecturer in the Smurfit Business School, UCD.

Claire Coughlan grew up in Co Kildare and graduated from UCD in 2002 with a BA in English and Italian. She has worked as a journalist since 2003 for publications such as the *Evening Herald* and *Irish Tatler* magazine. She is currently working on a novel which is set in 1920s Dublin.

Caroline Dowling lives and works in Co Kildare. Her poems have appeared in *The Stinging Fly* magazine. She is a recipient of the Tyrone Guthrie Bursary 2009 from Kildare County Council Arts Office. She is working on her first poetry collection.

Anne Graham is a UCD Arts graduate majoring in History and Greek and Roman Civilisation. She is currently working on a collection of short stories and a film script. She is also a singer-songwriter and artist. Anne currently resides in Wicklow.

Jennifer McGrath is a writer from Dublin with a strong family background in Wexford. She is a graduate of UCD, gaining a BA in English and Geography in 2007 as well as an MA in Drama and Performance Studies in 2008. She is a long standing member of the UCD English Literary Society and enjoys writing plays and short stories with a predilection for the comic, surreal and grotesque. Her story, 'The Black Swan', was chosen as one of the best stories of 2009 by Turner Maxwell books and her play, 'High School Reunion', was published in the ELS 2009 magazine *The Bell*. 'Boterique' was inspired by the painting *Man Goes to Work* by Fernando Botero.

Jamie O'Connell graduated from UCC in 2006 with a joint degree in English Literature and History of Art. He was shortlisted for the Wicklow Writers Short Story Award in 2008 and won the Thomas Harding Literary Award in 2006. He has written numerous book reviews and articles for various Irish publications. Two of his short stories were published in the ELS Anthology, *The Bell* (2009). He is a writer for the UCD *University Observer*.

Susan Stairs is a graduate of NCAD and has worked in the art business for many years. She has written and published three books on Irish art: *Markey Robinson – A Life*, *The Irish Figurists* and *Drawing from Memory – The Life of Irish Artist Gladys Maccabe*. Her work has been featured on Sunday Miscellany on RTÉ Radio in 2008 and 2009. Her short story, 'The Rescue', was one of the six stories shortlisted by US author Richard Ford for The Davy Byrnes Irish Writing Award 2009, from over 800 entries. She is currently working on a novel.

John Taylor has studied English and Creative Writing at Aberdeen University and UCD. 'Belfast Flâneur' is a collection of peripatetic and also stationary wanderings around cities, into the countryside and across borders. He is hoping over the next year to produce his first major work, to travel and to thoroughly enjoy himself.

Tania Tynan was born and raised in Co Wicklow. She graduated from NCAD with a joint honours degree in fine art painting and the history of art, and from DCU with an MA in film and TV studies. She has worked in film in Canada and taught Art and Media Studies in Irish schools. She writes children's and adults' fiction and has written screenplays. Her short story in this anthology is derived from her own experience of grief in its essence, but is largely imagined. She is currently living in Dublin and is working on a memoir of her mother.

Mariad Whisker was born in Belfast. She has a BA in Fashion and Textiles. She has lived between Dublin and Los Angeles and has studied Creative Writing at UCLA. Her career as a fashion designer has been put on ice while she pursues the MA at UCD. Her story 'Apache Territory' was short-listed for the Ian St James Award and published. In 2009, she was also short-listed for the Fish Publishing Prize in Flash Fiction for her short story, 'Something New'.